Contents

- Introduction.................... 4
- Rockfax Digital................. 6
- Symbol, Map and Topo Key........ 7
- Acknowledgments................. 8
- Rockfax Publications............10

- **Mallorca Logistics**...........12
  - When to Go and Getting There....14
  - Where to Stay..................16
  - Getting Around.................17
  - Shops, Tourist Info. and Guiding....18

- **Mallorca DWS**.................20
  - Access, Gear and Other Information. 22
  - Gear and Grades................24
  - Safety and Splashdowns.........25
  - Destination Planner............26

- **The Crags**....................28
  - Porto Cristo...................30
  - Porto Cristo Novo..............42
  - Cala Barques...................44
  - Cova des Burador...............58
  - Porto Colom....................62
  - Cala Marçal....................68
  - Cala Brafia....................76
  - Cala Estreta...................82
  - Cala Sa Nau....................86
  - Cala Mitjana...................96
  - Cala Serena...................106
  - Santanyí.....................126
  - Cala Llombards................134
  - Sa Calobra....................140
  - Port de Sóller................146
  - Porto Pi......................154

- **Route Index**..................156
- **Buttress Index**...............159
- **Map and General Index**........160

Oma Malk off *Rich Bitch* (6c+) - *p.98* - in the Rich Bitch Cave of Cala Mitjana. Photo: Mike Hutton

Mallorca has established itself as Europe's finest and most popular deep water soloing destination; many climbers come here just for this. The island's famous big golden pockets on steep overhanging walls of perfect rock are both enticing and intimidating. The splashdowns into the deep, warm blue water of the Mediterranean, followed by sangria and tapas at one of the island's many bars and restaurants, make the place all the more memorable. The height of the routes varies from a bouldery 5m to a terrifying 20m, and grades from 3+ to 9a+ mean that there is something here for everyone. Add all this together and it is not hard to see why this has become such a desirable destination.

The Book
This is the first dedicated 'printed' DWS book to Mallorca's magnificent deep water soloing but, in reality, it is Rockfax's eighth publication covering Mallorca DWS. First featured in PDF guides, it later got a chapter in the 2007 Rockfax guide Deep Water and then in all subsequent Mallorca Rockfax books. This new found independence gives more room to deliver even better information including bigger lavish photo-topos, aerial crag overviews and some spectacular action photography. This new edition also includes a hundred new climbs and a wealth of updated material.

Carrie Cooper on *Ejector Seat* (7c) - *p.36* - at Cova del Diablo, Porto Cristo. Photo: Jeff Rueppel

Rockfax Digital brings together over 50 guides from 4 publishers covering over 80,000 routes on 1600+ crags and presents it in a user-friendly package for use on mobile devices.

The heart of Rockfax Digital is the crag and route information covering 'areas' which roughly correspond to the printed guidebooks. The main data is sold by subscription so that you purchase access to everything for a period of time, from a month to a year. Once you are subscribed, you will have everything on Rockfax Digital for the duration. You can download the main data and store it on your device so you don't need any signal to be able to read the descriptions and see the topos and maps. There is plenty of free content available without a subscription, enabling you to get a really good impression of what Rockfax Digital is like without shelling out any money.

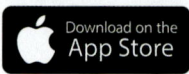
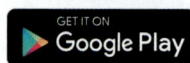

Rockfax Digital is available as an app which is free to download and incredibly useful in its own right. It contains a detailed crag map linked to the UKClimbing crags database with basic information and route lists for crags worldwide. The map also displays all the 3,800+ listings from the UKClimbing Directory of climbing walls, outdoor shops, climbing clubs, outdoor-specific accommodation and instructors and guides, amongst others.

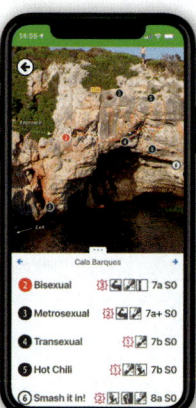

How to Subscribe to Rockfax Digital
Go to **rockfax.digital** to find links to download the app and create an account. New users can subscribe and get 7 days free.

Scan to find out more

UKC Logbooks
A popular method of logging your climbing is to use the **UKClimbing.com** logbooks system. This database has 653,000+ routes on over 24,700+ crags. So far, over 68,100 users have recorded more than 11 million ascents! To set up your own logbook, just register at **UKClimbing.com** and click on the logbook tab. You will be able to record every ascent you make, when you did it, what style you climbed it in and who you did it with. Each entry has a place for your own notes. You can also add your vote to the grade/star system which is used by guidebook writers to get opinions on grades and quality of routes. The logbook can be private, public or restricted to your own climbing partners only.

Rockfax Digital can be linked to your **UKClimbing.com** user account and logbook so that you can record your activity while at the crag. To do this you will need a 3G/4G/5G data connection. You can also look at the UKC logbooks to see if anyone has climbed your chosen route recently to check on conditions.

Symbol, Map and Topo Key — Mallorca Deep Water Soloing

Route Symbols

 A good route which is well worth the effort.

 A very good route, one of the best on the crag.

 A brilliant route, one of the best on the island.

 Technical climbing requiring good balance and technique, or complex and tricky moves.

 Powerful climbing; roofs, steep rock, low lock-offs or long moves off small holds.

 Sustained climbing; either lots of hard moves or steep rock giving pumpy climbing.

 Fingery climbing with significant small holds on the hard sections.

 Fluttery climbing with big fall potential and scary run-outs.

 A long reach is helpful, or even essential, for one or more of the moves.

 Some loose rock may be encountered.

 A dynamic move 'dyno' may well be needed.

Crag Symbols

 Angle of the approach walk to the crag with approximate time.

 Approximate time that the crag is in the direct sun (when it is shining).

 The crag can offer shelter from cold winds and it may be a good suntrap in colder weather.

 The crag suffers from seepage. It may well be wet and unclimbable in winter and early spring.

 An abseil approach is required. Not used on all crags where an abseil approach is possible.

 Deserted - Currently under-used and usually quiet. Fewer good routes or remote and smaller areas.

 Quiet - Less popular sections on major crags, or good buttresses with awkward approaches.

 Busy - Places you will seldom be alone, especially at weekends. Good routes and easy access.

 Crowded - The most popular sections of the most popular crags which are always busy.

Topo Key

Map Key

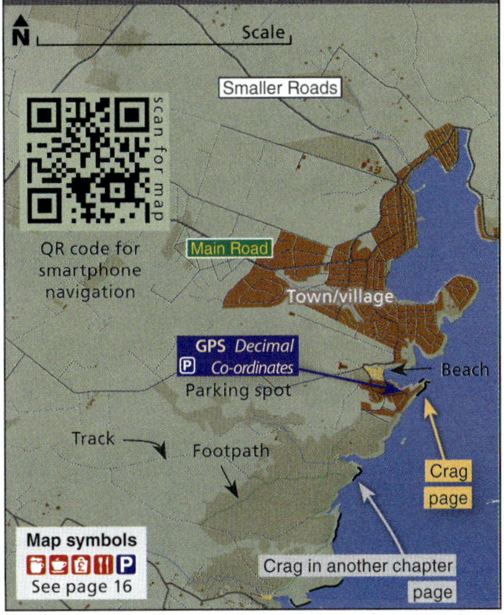

Mallorca Deep Water Soloing   Acknowledgments

8

Jess Carr on *Enter the Kraken* (6b+) - *p.102* - on the Kraken Wall, Cala Mitjana. Photo: Mike Hutton

Acknowledgments

2023 was the 20th anniversary of dedicated DWS trips for me. Over that time keen DWS explorers slowly added to the wealth of climbs now on offer and established Mallorca as the pre-eminent destination for the activity in Europe. Many thanks to all those who have contributed. Chief amongst these was Miquel Riera who sadly passed away in 2019. Miquel was a driving force behind climbing on the island and opened the doors for international recognition of Mallorca's DWS. I will always be very grateful for his hand-drawn topos and email communication back in the early days.

Thanks must be given to those past contributors who have been part of the evolution of this work - Toni Lamprecht, Chris Sharma, Ged Desforges, Alex Armitage, Mike Robertson, Ethan Pringle, Matt and Ben Heason, Sam Whittaker, Derek Watson, James Cole, Bernard Exley, Adam Brown, Tom Le Fanu, Delphine Byrne and all those who have sent in information, photos and comments over the years. A big thanks to those who have supplied specific information for this new edition with a particular mention to Julian Lines, Grant Farquhar, Frank Tetzel, Stephen Maginn, Bernard Boch, Felix Coxwell.

I would like to thank Mark Glaister for his additional crag photography in this book; Alan James for his editorial work and support throughout this guide and others over the years; and Rebecca Ting for her invaluable proof reading. Thanks also to the talented photographers - Jeff Rueppel, Mike Hutton, Matty Hong and Rasmus Kaessmann for their amazing action photography and also others who contributed action shots over the years. Thanks to the Rockfax technical developers, Stephen Horne, Martin McKenna, John McKenna and Paul Phillips and the rest of the UKC team.

Finally, thanks to Emma Harrington (now Emma Beail) for her incredibly valuable support, assistance, enthusiasm and passion for climbing. A big thank you to Theo for his patience while out and about on the island and bringing us much joy and laughter every day.

It's all massively appreciated and, as always, happy and safe soloing to you all!

Daimon Beail, April 2025

Advertisers

We are grateful to the following for supporting this guidebook.

BMC Insurance - Inside back cover
thebmc.co.uk/insurance

Rock and Water - Page 15
rockandwatermallorca.com

Rock On - Page 2
rockonclimbing.co.uk

Ròcodrom es cau - Back cover
rocodromescau.com

Rockfax Publications

North Wales Climbs
📖 March 2023
R+ October 2023

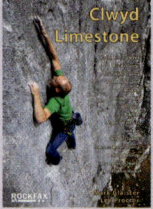

Clwyd Limestone
📖 December 2015
R+ December 2015

North Wales Slate
📖 September 2018
R+ March 2023

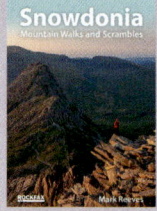

Snowdonia Scrambles
📖 December 2020
R December 2020

📖 Print version date
R Digital version date
R+ Digital has extra content

ROCKFAX digital

Scan to find out more

Order online from **rockfax.com**
30% discount for Rockfax Digital subscribers

South Wales Sport Climbs
📖 November 2024
R November 2024

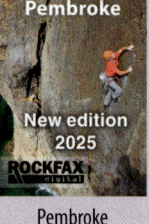

Pembroke
📖 August 2009
R+ April 2024

R Digital-only guides
North Wales Winter 2016
Gower Trad 2024

Austria and Switzerland
R Digital-only guides
Otztal (Austria) 2017
Eiger (Switzerland) 2016

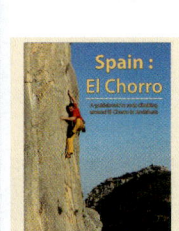

El Chorro
📖 December 2018
R December 2018

R Digital-only guides
Catalunya 2016
Madrid Area 2017
Sierra de Gredos 2024
Zaragoza 2016
Tenerife 2020
Northern Spain 2023

Greece and Cyprus
R Digital-only guides
Santorini 2019
Cyprus 2022

R Digital-only guides
Sasso Remenno 2019

Spain : Costa Blanca
📖 February 2013
R+ March 2023

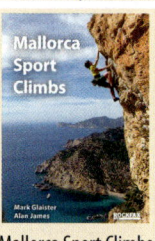

Mallorca Sport Climbs
📖 April 2025
R April 2025

Mallorca DWS
📖 April 2025
R April 2025

The Dolomites
📖 November 2019
R November 2019

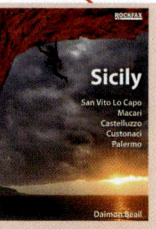

Sicily
📖 March 2021
R+ October 2023

Rockfax Publications

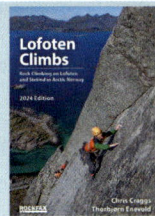
Lofoten Climbs
📖 May 2024
R May 2024

R Digital-only guides
Rjukan 2016
Nissedal 2016

SMC Digital-only guides
Scottish Rock Climbs 2024
Scottish Winter Climbs 2019
Highland Scrambles 2020
Available on the Rockfax App

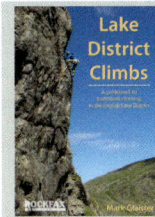
Lake District Climbs
📖 November 2019
R October 2023

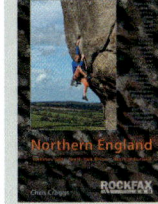
Northern England
📖 February 2008
R February 2008

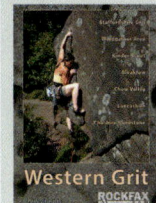
Western Grit
📖 April 2009
R June 2023

Northern Limestone
📖 January 2015
R+ June 2023

Eastern Grit
📖 May 2022
R+ August 2022

Peak Limestone
📖 June 2020
R+ October 2024

Peak Bouldering
📖 August 2023
R+ October 2023

West Country Climbs
📖 December 2022
R+ April 2023

Kalymnos
📖 May 2018
R+ April 2023

R Digital-only guides
Ailefroide 2021
Maurienne 2021

Southern Sandstone
📖 September 2017
R+ May 2023

Dorset
📖 July 2021
R+ October 2024

Dorset Bouldering
📖 May 2014
R+ January 2020

Devon Bouldering
📖 January 2024
R January 2024

For all trade printed book orders please direct enquiries to Cordee
Telephone: +44 145 561 1185   Email: info@cordee.co.uk
Trade Sales: sales@cordee.co.uk   Web: cordee.co.uk

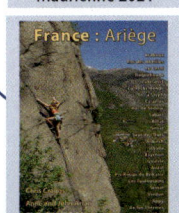
France : Ariege
📖 December 2012
R+ April 2021

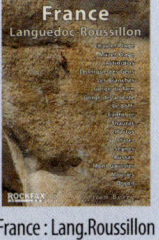
France : Lang.Roussillon
📖 November 2011
R November 2011

France : Haute Provence
📖 December 2009
R+ November 2022

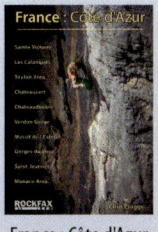
France : Côte d'Azur
📖 February 2017
R February 2017

Chamonix
📖 July 2022
R July 2022

Cala Barques is the paradise venue many think about when Mallorca DWS is mentioned. With challenging routes that are not too high, less experienced climbers can gain added confidence to give things a try. In this photo Rich Pollard is climbing *Metrosexual* (7a+) - *p.53* - at the Metrosexual Area. Most people tend to start from a half-height ledge but the original route from 2003 started from lower down, just above the water. Photo: Mike Hutton

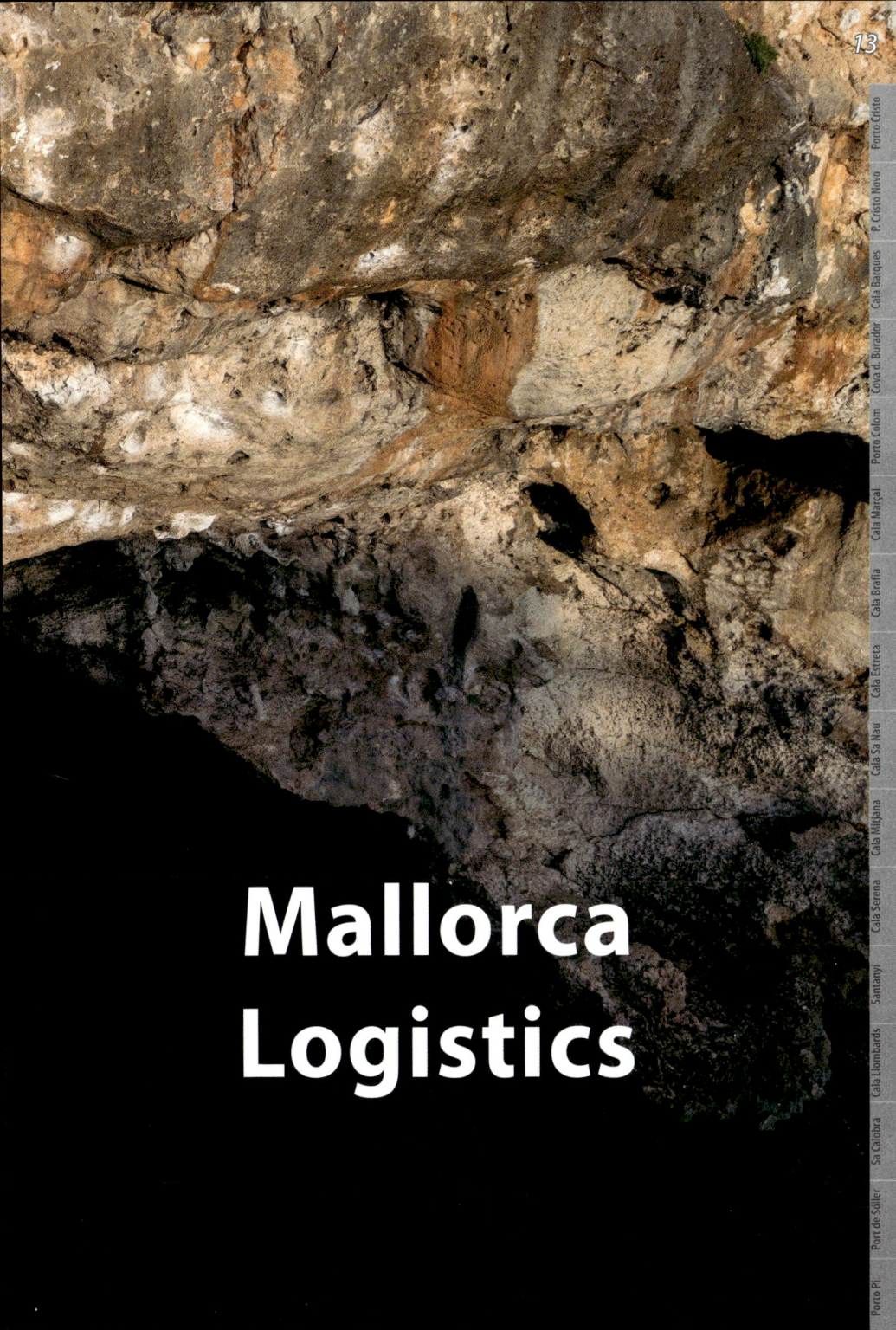

Mallorca Logistics

When to Go

The most popular time for climbers to visit Mallorca tends to be September and October when the sea is still warm and the average air temperature is in the mid-to-low 20s. Late October can be the wet time of the year but it is still possible to dodge the showers. November is also a good possibility but it can be cooler which can lead to good conditions especially for the steeper and harder climbs. April to June is closer to British summer DWS conditions but most may want to bring a wetsuit for added comfort when in the water.

Some of the local climbers see July and August as a prime time to go soloing, but for many this will be far too hot to actually climb. Jellyfish are most abundant in July, which is another reason to stay away at that time.

Mallorca Averages	Jan	Feb	Mar	Apr	May	Jun	Jul	Aug	Sep	Oct	Nov	Dec
Temperature (maximum)	10	15	17	19	22	26	29	29	27	23	18	15
Temperature (minimum)	6	6	8	10	18	17	19	20	18	14	10	8
Hours of sunshine	5	6	7	8	10	11	12	11	8	6	6	4
Sea Temperature	14	13	14	15	17	19	24	25	24	21	18	15
Rainfall in mm / month	40	32	35	30	7	10	5	6	61	73	60	50
Wet days (>0.1mm) / month	8	6	8	5	5	3	1	3	6	9	8	9

Getting There by Air

Mallorca's international airport is on the outskirts of the city of Palma and is on the destination list of many airlines. This means bargain flights at off-peak times and reasonable value ones at popular times, with the added advantage of being able to book outward and return flights separately.

Getting There Without Flying

It is possible to get to the island without flying, although it is time consuming. There are ferries from Valencia, Dénia (on the Costa Blanca) and Barcelona to Palma, and from Barcelona to Port d'Alcúdia. The high speed AVE railway serves Valencia and Barcelona.

Travel Insurance

It is strongly advised that travel, medical and rescue insurance is taken out before undertaking a trip. If you are in any doubt, just ask someone who has had cause to use it!

BMC Travel Insurance   *Inside back cover*
services.thebmc.co.uk/insurance

Guidebook Footnote

The inclusion of a climbing area in this guidebook does not mean that you have a right of access or the right to climb upon it. The descriptions of routes within this guide are recorded for historical reasons only and no reliance should be placed on the accuracy of the description. The grades set in this guide are a fair assessment of the difficulty of the climbs. Climbers who attempt a route of a particular standard should use their own judgment as to whether they are proficient enough to tackle that route. This book is not a substitute for experience and proper judgment. The authors, publisher and distributors of this book do not recognise any liability for injury or damage caused to, or by, climbers, third parties, or property arising from such persons seeking reliance on this guidebook as an assurance for their own safety.

Mallorca Logistics — Where to Stay

Where to Stay

The most popular option for accommodation in Mallorca is to take advantage of the villas and apartments designed for the busy summer tourist trade. For DWS it is best to look at the east coast, but there is plenty available all across the island and being more centrally placed will cut down travel time if combining roped and unroped activities.

This Map
- Airport
- Ferry
- Hospital
- Gear Shop
- Climbing Wall

Other Maps
- Bar
- Cafe
- Restaurant
- Supermarket
- Chemist
- Parking

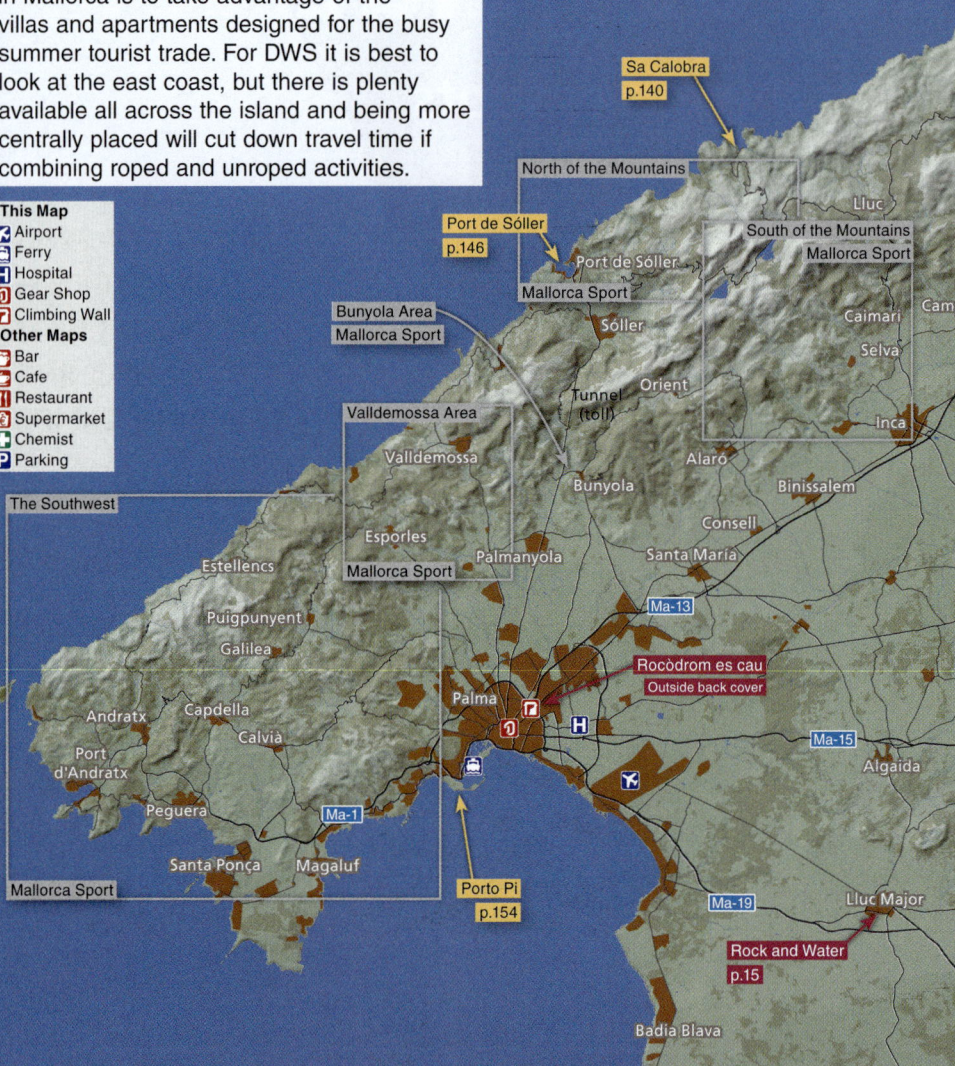

Hiring a villa is an attractive option, especially for those in a large group (6 to 10). There are also plenty of apartments available that offer good value for couples and small groups. The best place to find companies who offer accommodation is to type 'Mallorca accommodation' or 'Majorca accommodation' into Google.

Getting Around — Mallorca Logistics

Getting Around

With a Car - A hire car is advisable for deep water soloing trips on Mallorca since you will not be able to get the most out of a trip without access to one. The crag approaches are written assuming you have access to a car.

Without a Car - There is public transport from Palma but using it will usually require a long walk, or a difficult hitch, to get to the crag. The tourist information offices have good information about bus services which nearly all depart from the area around the train stations.

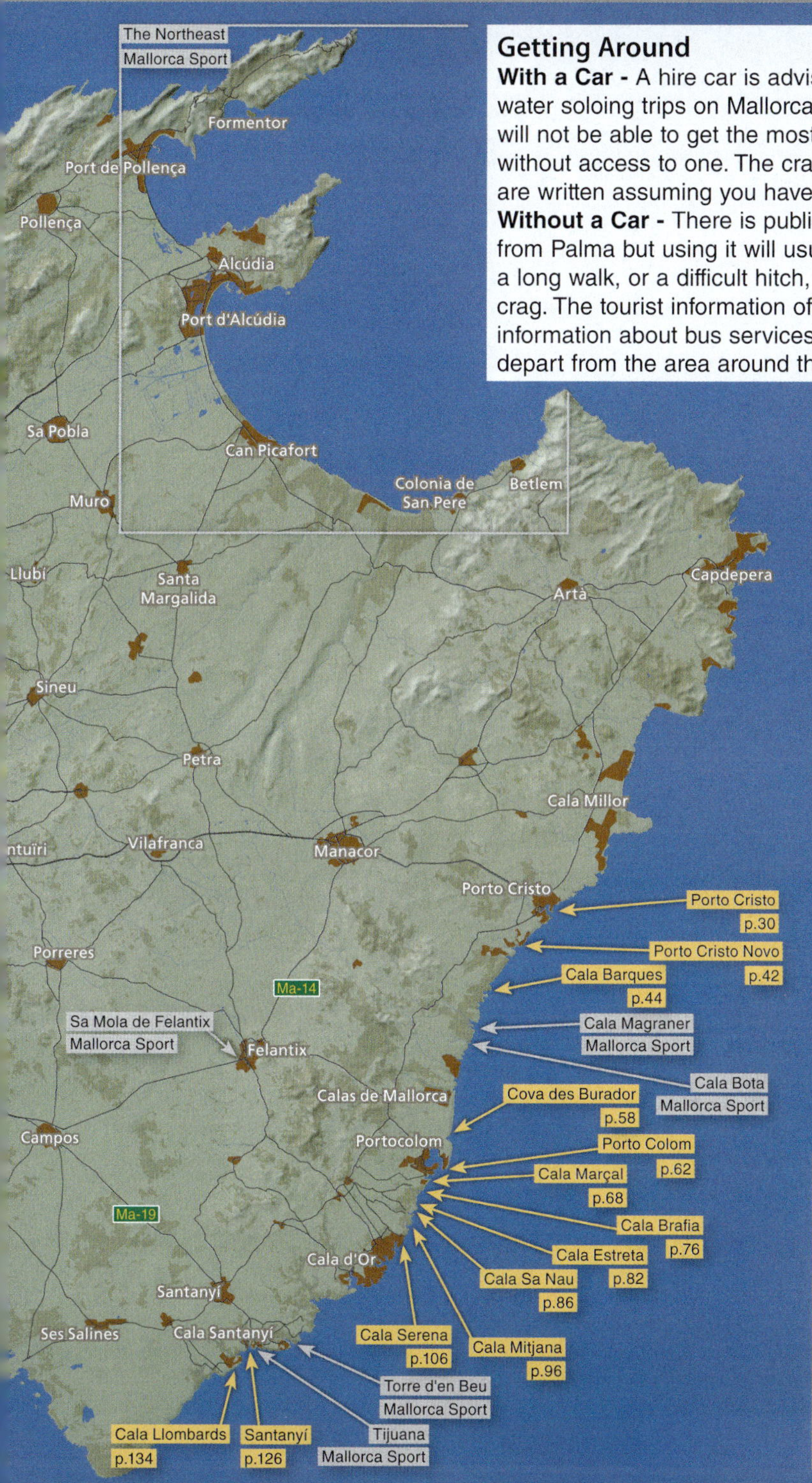

- The Northeast — Mallorca Sport
- Sa Mola de Felantix — Mallorca Sport
- Porto Cristo — p.30
- Porto Cristo Novo — p.42
- Cala Barques — p.44
- Cala Magraner — Mallorca Sport
- Cala Bota — Mallorca Sport
- Cova des Burador — p.58
- Porto Colom — p.62
- Cala Marçal — p.68
- Cala Brafia — p.76
- Cala Estreta — p.82
- Cala Sa Nau — p.86
- Cala Serena — p.106
- Cala Mitjana — p.96
- Torre d'en Beu — Mallorca Sport
- Tijuana — Mallorca Sport
- Santanyí — p.126
- Cala Llombards — p.134

Mallorca Sport Climbs
Mark Glaister, Alan James
📖 April 2025
Ⓡ April 2025

Daila Ojeda on *Metrosexual* (7a+) - *p.53* - Cala Braques. Photo: Jeff Rueppel

Tourist Information Offices
Mallorca has almost 50 tourist information offices across the island with two main offices located at the airport and in Palma. For a full list visit:
mallorca.es/en/tourist-information-offices

Shops
There are large supermarkets in most of the major towns and hypermarkets in Palma. Opening times for the majority of shops in Mallorca are from 10am to 1:30pm and 4pm to 8pm. Most supermarkets stay open during the whole day and open a lot earlier. Most shops will be shut on national holidays and many, but not all, will be shut on Sundays.

Climbing Shops
There are several climbing shops that sell climbing gear on the island plus a couple of Decathlons on the outskirts of Palma. You can also get your climbing shoes resoled.

Foracorda - Specialist climbing shop in Palma with the best brands. **foracorda.com**

Guiding Services
If you are after a guide for all types of climbing then here are some options:

Rock and Water   *Page 15*
Web: rockandwatermallorca.com
Tel: +34 619 751 515
Email: info@rockandwatermallorca.com

Ròcodrom es cau - Offer outdoor and indoor climbing courses - see below.

Climbing Walls
Of course the weather on Mallorca is always perfect, right? Well not always, in which case you may want to make use one of the local climbing walls.

Ròcodrom es cau   *Outside back cover*
C/ Jaume Ferran No. 72, Palma
Web: rocodromescau.com
Tel: +34 648 704 717
Email: rocodromescau@gmail.com

Mallorca DWS

British DWS pioneer Ken Palmer topping out on *Rich Bitch* (6c+) - *p.98* - at the Rich Bitch Cave at Cala Mitjana. Photo: Mike Hutton

Access

Access is an extremely sensitive issue on Mallorca. Access to some DWS and sport climbing crags has been lost because of a variety of problems. Sometimes it is because of uncooperative landowners, but frequently it is caused by a lack of respect by climbers and their impact on the environment, specifically related to bad parking and ignoring the 'leave no trace' ethic. There are other crags contained within this guidebook that could easily go the same way if climbers are not careful with how they access and behave at climbing areas. Always park considerately, remove all litter, keep noise to a minimum, no fires, fly camping and ensure you use the correct approach paths as described in this guide. Be aware that approaches may change, so check for updated information available on Rockfax Digital and follow local signs if the information is different to that included in this book.

DWS Gear

What to take? In late September and early October - not a lot. The water is so warm that there is no need for a wet-uit. You can get by with two pairs of boots and a few chalk bags. Take plenty of chalk and sandwich bags to line the inside of your chalk bag for when it gets wet. Alternatively, find an old chalk bag and rip the fleece liner out of it. Liquid chalk is also a good option. A dinghy is essential for some routes which are otherwise inaccessible. Inflatable boats can be picked up from tourist hot spots cheaply. It is strongly advised to install a water exit at every venue to enable a safe way out of the water. Take a rope, or rope-ladder, specifically for water exits and purchase a rubber ring with handles to attach to the exit rope incase you need it. A 30m rope is needed for a few venues, as are a few slings for accessing the base of some of the climbs.

Conditions and Tides

There is a small tidal range but it is of no significance on any of the crags covered in this book. Please be aware of possible currents while swimming under crags - see the section on safety on p.25. Some of Mallorca's crags are prone to condensation especially in the summer. This is caused by a combination of high temperatures, lack of a sea breeze and crags that are often too steep to receive the high summer sun. If you find a crag in these conditions then head for one of the less overhanging venues which could well be dry and climbable. The crags can sometimes be plagued by jellyfish. The big ones (*mild rhizostoma pulmo*) are easy to spot and normally stay away from the crags, or drift away quickly on the tide. The smaller grey jellyfish (*pelagia noctiluca*) travel around in shoals, drifting on the currents. Occasionally hundreds have been seen at a crag and many climbers have been stung a few times, however, you don't see jellyfish all the time and it's quite possible for you to spend a week or two in Mallorca and not see any at all.

New Routes and Other Areas

This Rockfax guide offers the best available coverage of the island's recorded DWS climbs. The nature of the coastline means that there is lots of potential for new climbs. Some smaller isolated locations only have a few climbs recorded and thus have not been included at this time. One key area of development is the Northwest coast which is seeing some of the hardest DWS climbs anywhere, mostly by Chris Sharma. Development of these areas is in its infancy, the areas are very remote and access is primarily from a boat or other more challenging method. These crags have not been included at this time.

If you climb a new route, or develop an area, then record it with as much information as possible and submit it to UKC Logbooks (p.6). This is the best way to ensure that we find out about your new climb for possible inclusion in future guides. Ongoing updates will be added to the Rockfax Digital (p.6) version of the climbing information in this book between editions.

Mallorca DWS 23

One of the finest hard solos on the island - *Animal Magnetism* (8b+) - *p.101* - on the Wall of Illuminations at Cala Mitjana. Photo: Mike Hutton

Grades

The DWS routes on Mallorca are graded using the familiar sport grade. Mallorcan grades have had a reputation over the years for being extremely hard, especially in the range from 5a to around 7a, although this is less of a problem with the DWS routes. Through successive Rockfax guidebooks, and the voting on UKClimbing logbooks, we have tried to rationalise the grades, bringing them into line with other areas, but there may still be the odd surprise out there.

Colour Coding

The routes are colour coded corresponding to a grade band:
Green Spots *Beginners* - everything at grade 4c and under. There aren't many DWS routes in this band.
Orange Spots *Experienced* - 5a to 6a+ inclusive. General ticking routes.
Red Spots *Advanced* - 6b to 7a inclusive. The next level routes to push yourself on.
Black Spots *Expert* - 7a+ to 7c+. Hard routes for dedicated deep water soloists.
White Spots *Elite* - 8a and above. The hardest routes for the World's best climbers.

Sport Grade	British Trad Grade (for well-protected routes)	UIAA	USA
1	Mod (Moderate)	I	5.1
2	Diff (Difficult)	II	5.2
2+		III-	5.3
3a	VDiff (Very Difficult)	III	5.4
3b	HVD (Hard Very Difficult)	III	5.4
3c	Sev (Severe)	III+	5.5
4a	HS (Hard Severe)	IV-	5.6
4b	VS (Very Severe)	IV	5.7
4c		IV+	5.8
5a	HVS (Hard Very Severe)	V-	5.8
5b		V	5.9
5c	E1	V+	5.9
6a	E2	VI-	5.10a
6a+		VI	5.10b
6b	E3	VI+	5.10c
6b+		VII-	5.10d
6c	E4	VII	5.11a
6c+		VII+	5.11b
7a	E5	VIII-	5.11c
7a+		VIII	5.11d
7b	E6	VIII+	5.12a
7b+		IX-	5.12b
7c	E7	IX	5.12c
7c+		IX	5.12d
8a	E8	IX+	5.13a
8a+		X-	5.13b
8b	E9	X	5.13c
8b+		X	5.13d
8c	E10	X+	5.14a
8c+		XI-	5.14b
9a	E11	XI	5.14c
9a+		XI+	5.14d
			5.15a

S Grades

All grades are presented in a dual format. Sport grades give the technical aspect of the route and the S-grade indicates the general impression of what it's like to solo the route.

S0 = Safe and relatively non-committing. Usually with a low crux move and clean falls into the water.

S1 = The routes are higher, making the falls a bit more serious.

S2 = Higher routes with longer falls but may also have protruding ledges above or below the water. The water may be shallow in places, making it a lot more committing, and bailing out will require a bit of precision to get into the water safely.

S3 = Often with high cruxes, above shallow water, exposed and genuinely dangerous. Take great care - many of these routes are not safe to fall from!

Safety and Splashdowns — Mallorca DWS

Setting up exit points and safety before setting out at Cala Serena. Photo: Beail Collection

Safety

> Be a confident and strong swimmer.
> Always climb in teams of two or more.
> Never solo alone and do not rely on climbers you do not know to be your safety spotter.
> Be sure that you can get out of the water by means of a rope or an easy exit.
> Take a flotation device which can be used in a rescue or alternatively for rests in the water.
> Avoid climbing when there are medium or large swells and know your limits.
> Take a first aid kit and know how to use it.
> Be safe, enjoy yourself, in emergencies call 112 and make sure you are appropriately insured.

Splashdowns

Develop and practise the skill of splashdowns - hitting the water wrong from a height can result in being winded, wounded (broken ribs) or an enema. Practising by jumping from clifftops is not advised. When climbing you will usually be way below this point and falling off the rock face - skills to safely 'eject' yourself are key. For a normal splashdown into deep water, stay loose all the way down and then assume a good entry position in the last few metres of the fall (or jump). This initial looseness of the body is important, as it prevents the body tightening which often results in an off-kilter landing. It's also worth remembering that 'wheeling' your outstretched arms in small circles provides a way of rotating the body forwards or backwards. Upon entry, keep your arms tight against your body and your head upright (don't look down - you'll get a face-full). And don't forget to shut your legs! If falling from low down and for most smaller cliffs, a chair style landing is fine. A bit of chop in the sea, or a small swell where waves break against the rock and inject air into the sea helps break the surface and make landing in the water much softer. Remember a flat water surface can be as hard as concrete if hit wrongly.

DWS Destination Planner

	Routes	up to 4c	5a to 6a+	6b to 7a	7a+ to 7c+	8a and up
East Coast						
Porto Cristo	58	1	16	13	19	9
Porto Cristo Novo	8	-	1	5	1	1
Cala Barques	66	-	7	27	23	9
Cova des Burador	13	-	4	9	-	-
Porto Colom	22	-	-	9	13	-
Cala Marçal	26	2	17	7	-	-
Cala Brafia	20	-	9	8	3	-
Cala Estreta	11	1	2	4	2	2
Cala Sa Nau	29	3	7	10	5	4
Cala Mitjana	35	-	9	12	7	7
Cala Serena	126	-	22	88	15	1
Santanyí	22	1	9	5	2	5
Cala Llombards	11	-	1	4	2	4
Rest of Island						
Sa Calobra	11	-	4	6	1	-
Port de Sóller	21	3	3	13	2	-
Porto Pi	11	-	5	4	1	1
Route Totals	490	11	116	224	96	43

Approach	Sun	Shelt-ered	Seep-age	Abseil In	Summary	Page	
2 min	Lots of sun				The world's most iconic deep water soloing venue. Diablo's steep, pocketed walls tower to a challenging 18m above the sea, and offer a variety of high-quality testpieces. Close by is the magnificent Tower of Falcons.	30	Porto Cristo
8 min	Lots of sun		Seepage		An amazing stalactite-ridden cave offering few lines, but without question a wealth of possibilities. An area for the more dedicated soloer.	41	P. Cristo Novo
55 - 60 min	Lots of sun				The most popular and idyllic deep water soloing crag, offering a unique playground of small caves and overhanging walls, with the added attraction of the fearsome Tarantino Cave.	46	Cala Barques
10 - 18 min	Morning				A connoisseur's crag with high walls, a lengthy traverse and a limited number of climbs. The Dominion Wall offers the best here.	57	Cova d. Burador
15 min	Sun and shade	Sheltered			A fantastic venue popularised by the shorter roof-climbs on the lower wall. Being in a sheltered cove is an added bonus.	62	Porto Colom
1 - 2 min	Morning	Sheltered			An excellent choice for anyone wanting a bit more length to their climbs, with plenty in the low to mid-grades. Easy access, and a great afternoon spot.	68	Cala Marçal
15 min	Morning				A nice cliff which features a number of routes which start from a mid-height break. A number of short lines can also be found in the bay.	76	Cala Brafia
25 min	Sun and shade				A realm of extreme possibilities overshadowed by a gigantic roof. One almighty line up its centre and more attainable lines on the wings.	82	Cala Estreta
5 - 14 min	Morning	Sheltered			A giant cave with fierce, cutting-edge lines in the high grades. In complete contrast is the Virgin Area, which offers a friendly introduction to DWS, while the Bay Area offers a number of great and popular traverses.	86	Cala Sa Nau
25 min	Morning	Sheltered			Home to a small number of the island's classics, and normally visited on the same day as Cala Sa Nau. Four areas each with their own characteristics, including a popular little cave offering plenty of fun lines.	96	Cala Mitjana
2 - 22 min	Morning		Seepage		The biggest venue on the island with a ton of climbs. Golden, juggy walls low down are generally followed by thinner, technical sections above. Most routes are an ideal height.	108	Cala Serena
5 - 10 min	Sun and shade				Short and mostly easy routes located close to the sport climbing at Tijuana. Nearby is the spectacular Es Pontas arch and its famous hard climb which goes by the same name.	126	Santanyi
15 - 30 min	To mid afternoon			Abseil In	Two isolated venues which have proven popular with the elite. The routes are mostly in the higher grades, and tackle steep caves and thin upper walls.	135	Cala Llombards
15 - 20 min	Afternoon				An area of outstanding natural beauty and a popular tourist destination. Features some good novelty climbs around the mouth of the Torrent de Pareis and some very public climbs at the well-named Arena. It can get busy in the holiday season.	140	Sa Calobra
20 - 50 min	Morning		Seepage		Two distinct DWS areas - the Bay Area with plenty of climbs to suit the first time DWS climber and those seeking lower-grade climbs, and Cova de Ses Puntes with its wild and exposed harder cave climbs.	146	Port de Soller
2 min	Lots of sun				A small but popular venue situated near Palma's shipping docks. This is an ideal spot for island arrival days or a last-minute climb before catching the plane home. The historical home to the first solos on the island.	153	Porto Pi

Faded symbol means only some of the routes are affected by the symbol characteristic

The Crags

Andrew Chapman on *Chapman* (6a+) - *p.48* - at the Cova Area of Cala Barques. Photo: Beail Collection

Chris Savage on *Life is too Short to Spend it on Cheap Champagne* (7c) - *p.36* - at Cova del Diablo, Porto Cristo. Photo: Mike Hutton

The main crag at Porto Cristo is Cova del Diablo, arguably the World's most popular DWS venue which put Mallorca at the epicentre of it all. This overhanging limestone amphitheatre, which rises to 18m above the sea, is covered in pockets, jugs and tufas. The edges of the crags also have a number of more vertical challenges at lower grades to enjoy. The venue can be a little high for some although usually the crux moves are less than two-thirds height but it may feel higher than this depending on the route you are on.

Some featured stars of Diablo are *The Lobster*, *Afroman* and *Loskot and Two Smoking Barrels* with its incredible dynamic move, seen in many a video. There are also some worthwhile yet little travelled lines in the outlying areas. Many get to grips with the venue by indulging in some of the great traverses. *White Noise* when travelling from right to left can lead into *Superwoman* for perhaps one of the best DWS traverses found anywhere.

Porto Cristo
P. Cristo Novo
Cala Barques
Cova d. Burador
Porto Colom
Cala Marçal
Cala Brafia
Cala Estreta
Cala Sa Nau
Cala Mitjana
Cala Serena
Santanyi
Cala Llombards
Sa Calobra
Port de Sóller
Porto Pi

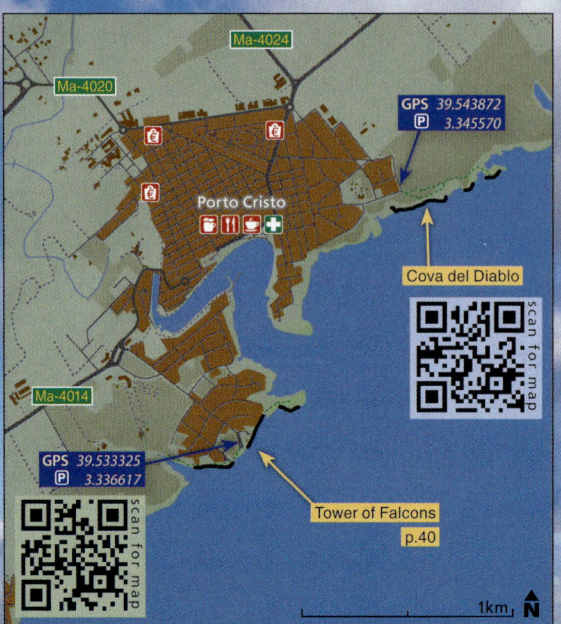

Approach

Cova del Diablo is on the edge of the small town of Porto Cristo. From Manacor, take the Ma-4020 road to Porto Cristo. On the edge of town, turn left at the first roundabout onto Ronda de l'Oest and follow this to the next roundabout. Take the second exit here and very shortly after, turn left onto Carrer de la Proa and follow this round to the right. Continue to the junction with Avinguda Cala Petita and turn left onto it. Follow this road to the edge of the town as it bends around towards the sea. Park on the corner nearest the sea (removing all valuables from your car) and take a short walk through some bushes to the cliff edge. You can also reach this point from the town centre navigating through the one-way system. For **Tower of Falcons** approach see p.40.

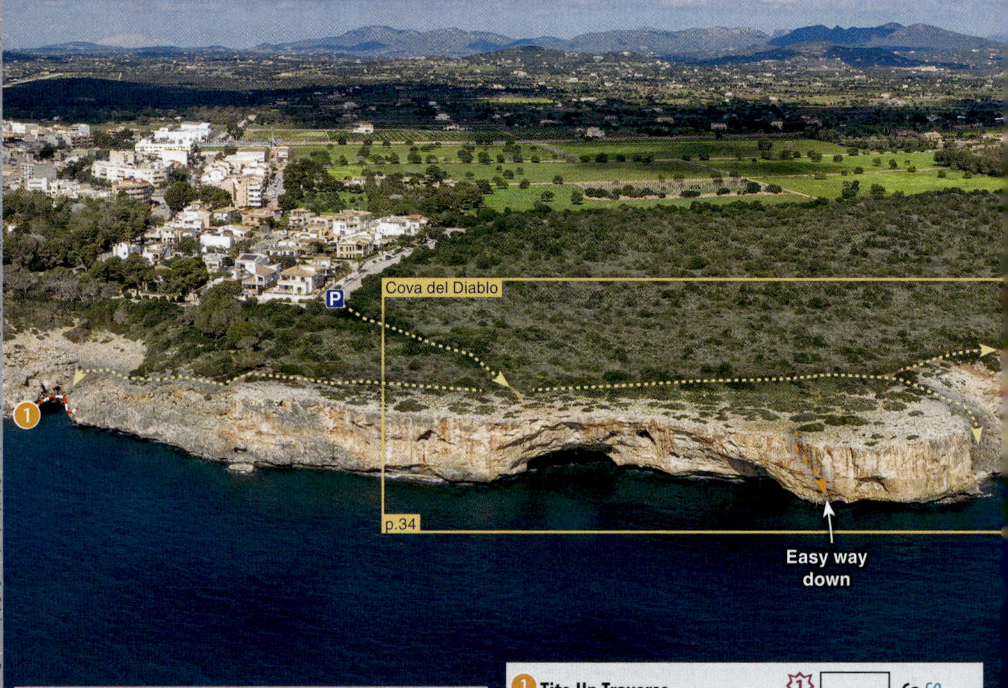

Cova del Diablo - Outlying

There are three outlying routes located to either side of the main Diablo area which are of interest.

Exit - For *Tits-Up Traverse*, climb only when the sea is calm and exit where possible - rope advised. For *Big Bully* and *The Voyage*, exit onto the boulder beach.

1 Tits-Up Traverse .... 1 ☐ **6a** *S0*

Slightly further west along the coast, where the mighty Diablo fades away, is a small cut-out basin with this small left-to-right traverse. A combination of pebble-dash, quartz and other strange minerals make this worth a visit. A slight extension up the bulging prow at the end gives a nice finish.

FA. Kirilee Wood, Lauren Matthews 10.2001

Porto Cristo

Conditions
The crag faces south to southeast and can get a lot of sun, so it stays fairly dry most of the time. The holds are generally in good condition but in some places (more specifically on the traverses) they are becoming polished. There is not much seepage, but the cove occasionally experiences damp conditions, which can sometimes put the crag out of action for days. This is mostly caused by humidity. The crag also has another downside apart from the soakings, which is the abundance of bird poo. This is mostly found in the caves and on some of the larger ledges. The caves also attract mosquitoes.

Water Exits
There have been problems with the exit from the water at Diablo when the sea is rough. The landing platform exit along to the northeast is the easiest but can sometimes become a no-go area in rough or choppy seas. Efforts made to ease your exit from the water are essential precautions. There are usually fixed ropes in place (though these should be removed after use). Best to set up your own and ensure it works for you, especially at the bottom of the easy way down. Alternative exits (although not ones which enable you to reach the top of the crag) are found along the crag - the key ones are under *The Lobster*, as well as the very intense exit under the cave of *Afroman*.

❷ **Big Bully** .... 6a+ *S3*
Walk past the boulder beach eastwards for about 100m. Then carefully make your way down to a smaller boulder beach and head to the right side of the bay (looking out). Traverse out onto the steeper part of the buttress. The line starts at a cut-out section at the base of the cliff. Take care on this one as a protruding prow down to the right is waiting to catch your fall - aim carefully if bailing out!
FA Mike Robertson 10.2001

❸ **The Voyage** 6a *S0*
A long traverse over very safe ground and on great holds. This route is on the isolated headland further east along the coast. Start at the left (looking out) side and traverse along the slightly overhanging wall until you reach an easy groove after about 50m. Exit up an easy groove to finish.
FA Mike Robertson 10.2001

Porto Cristo — Cova del Diablo - Surfing Bird Area

Lots of sun — 2 hr

Labels on photo: Way down, 18m, 18m, Superwoman p.37, Water exit rope can be installed here, routes ①②③④⑤⑥⑦

Cova del Diablo - Surfing Bird Area

This left (west) end of the crag provides a good selection of grades, and the finish of the girdle of *Superwoman*. The rock has some huge pockets and buckets. Wait for a calm sea. Avoid climbing here when the rock is damp, which it often is in the summer when the sun is high.

Approach - Left side (map and overview p.32) - The first four routes are reached by a rope-assisted down-climb or abseil. *Surfing Bird* requires an abseil into its niche start, or a tricky traverse round. *Blue Tuna* and *Let's Have It* are best approached by dry-bag swim or boat, or by a traverse from the left and then a crawl along the ledge.

Approach - Centre-left - To reach the starts of *Iguanodon* to *Surfing in the Bar*, traverse leftwards (looking in) along *Superwoman* and then drop down into the lower cave. The upper wall routes (above *Iguanodon*) *Microdot*, through to *Beware of Limbo Dancers* are normally reached via the line of *Superwoman* or as extensions to *Iguanodon*.

❶ You toucha my car, I breaka your face
.... 6a+ *S1*
The slab left of *The Italian Job*.
FA. Bernard Boch 9.2014

❷ The Italian Job 6b *S1*
Climb the wall and then overhanging ground on the left edge of the main Diablo amphitheatre, using huge holds and massive pockets. The crux is at mid-height, above an easier diagonal feature that takes you rightwards to the top.
FA. Mike Robertson 10.2001

❸ Swing Both Ways 6c *S1*
A harder alternative to the above route, swinging right onto slightly more powerful ground in the bulging mid-section. Finish as for *The Italian Job*.
FA. Neil Gresham 10.2001

❹ Liv 7a *S1*
A fine line which touches *Surfing Bird* at the overhang bulge. Continue direct via jugs and finish up the golden streak. It is also possible to finish left as for *The Italian Job*.
FA. Bernard Boch 9.2014

❺ Surfing Bird 7b *S1*
The first of the late Miquel Riera's classics from his early wave of development. From the lower ledge take the red/cream streak up through bold ground onto the higher bulge and the top.
FA. Miquel Riera, Pepino Lopez and Xisco Meca, late 1980s

❻ Blue Tuna .... 6c+ *S2*
A great slice of climbing. From the left edge of the low cave, climb powerfully through the roof (crux) and follow the biggest holds all the way to the top.
FA. Julian Lines 9.2002

❼ Let's Have It! .... 7c+ *S2*
Start in the centre of the low/left sea-level cave at the very edge of the water itself, taking care with water depth early on. Climb up and continue to the big half-height recess, passing a crux slap for a two-finger pocket.
FA. Klem Loskot 10.2001

Cova del Diablo - Surfing Bird Area — Porto Cristo

8 Iguanodon 7b S0
Super steep though often greasy climbing, heading leftwards along a juggy rail. If the pump does not get you then you either jump when finished or head left along *Superwoman*, with extra points if you have a go at one of the upper wall routes.
FA. Neil Gresham 10.2001

9 Microdot 7b S3
An extension to the lower routes gives some high and feisty moves pulling through into the top recess. For the brave only.
FA. Neil Gresham 9.2002

10 Dancing Fool 7c S2
Climb the wall to the right of the cave until you reach a horizontal crack. Now continue slightly leftwards with long powerful moves to the top.
FA. Toni Lamprecht 2006

11 Beware of Limbo Dancers 8a+ S2
From the top of *Iguanodon*, traverse rightwards and use small holds to gain a crack system. The bouldery crux comes on the orange section of the wall but the real kick is in the top-out.
FA. Toni Lamprecht 2006

12 Dancing Limbo in Sunshine
.... 8b S3
Link *If You Keep Your Face...* into *Beware of Limbo Dancers*.
FA. Philipp Geisenhoff 2022

13 Surfing in the Shadow
.... 8a+ S2
Midway up the face, from any line you like, climb through a distinct undercut and pockets above to then borrow the tufa on the left and finish over to the right as for *Surfing in the Bar*.
FA. Nils Favre 2021

14 If You Keep Your Face in the Sunshine, You Will Not See the Shadow 8b S3
A very steep and sought-after prize here at Diablo. Start a few metres right of *Iguanodon*, and climb the steep wall to reach a small cave at half height. From the cave, climb the rest of the line direct to the final bulge at the top.
FA. Klem Loskot 2002

15 Surfing in the Bar. 7a S2
Attack the steep wall to a sit-down rest in the cave. From here, an airy finale up the top face is your ticket to ride.
FA. Miquel Riera late 1980s

16 Hip Hop .... 7b+ S2
The streaked wall up and left of the big cave. Climb the left edge of the cave and sprint to the top.
FA. Miquel Riera 2002

17 Surfer Dead .... 6c+ S2
Negotiate the right-hand edge of the big central cave, then move rightwards up the very steep top face - keep well right of the big hanging tufa. Save some energy for the pumpy top crux, as there aren't many footholds.
FA. Miquel Riera late 1980s

18 Sea Devil 7a S2
The right-hand side of the enticing orange streaks.
FA. Grant Farquhar 2002. Also claimed by Klem Mai in 2002 as *Rescate Emocional*.

Porto Cristo — Cova del Diablo - The Lobster Area

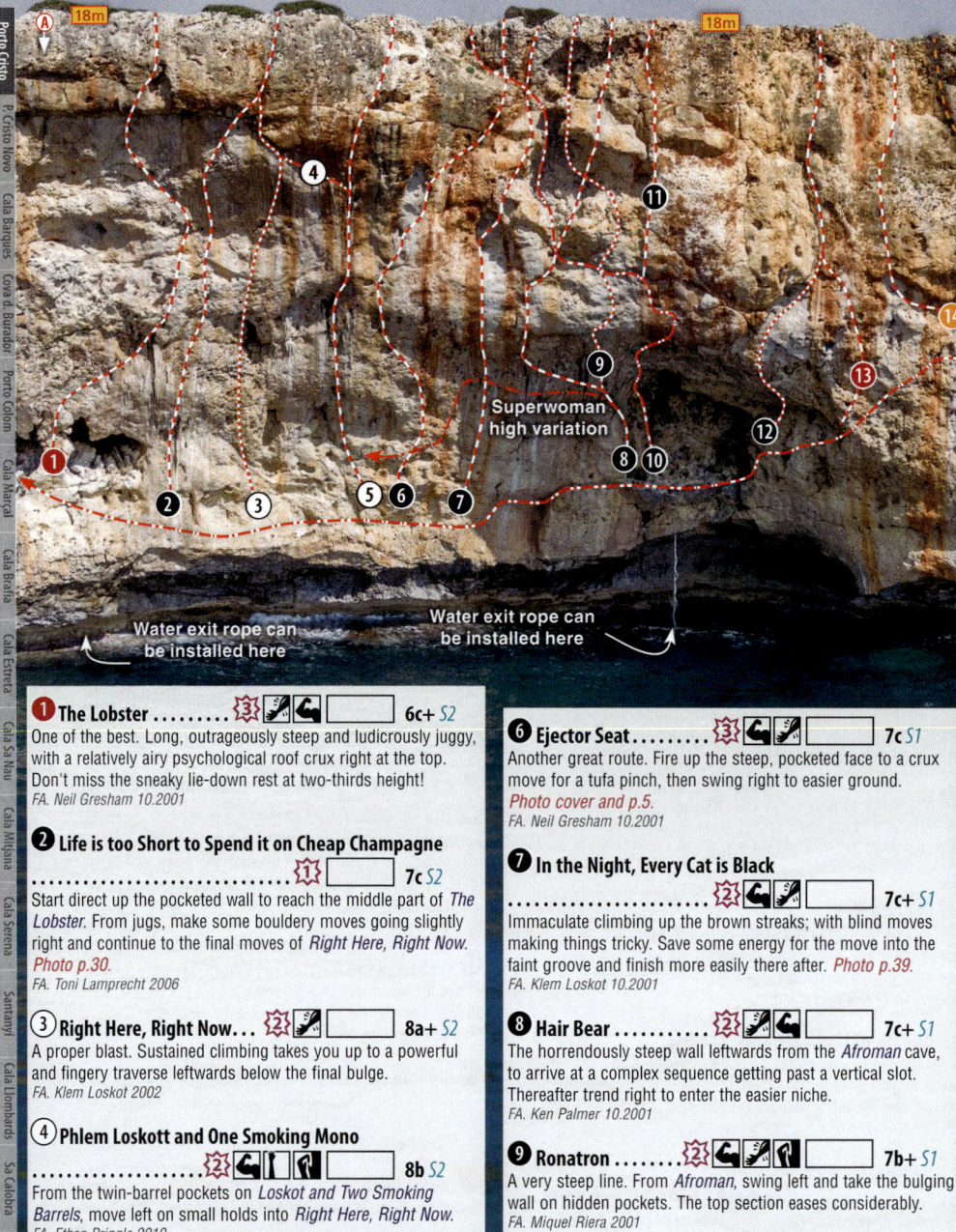

❶ The Lobster — 6c+ S2
One of the best. Long, outrageously steep and ludicrously juggy, with a relatively airy psychological roof crux right at the top. Don't miss the sneaky lie-down rest at two-thirds height!
FA. Neil Gresham 10.2001

❷ Life is too Short to Spend it on Cheap Champagne — 7c S2
Start direct up the pocketed wall to reach the middle part of *The Lobster*. From jugs, make some bouldery moves going slightly right and continue to the final moves of *Right Here, Right Now*. *Photo p.30.*
FA. Toni Lamprecht 2006

❸ Right Here, Right Now... — 8a+ S2
A proper blast. Sustained climbing takes you up to a powerful and fingery traverse leftwards below the final bulge.
FA. Klem Loskot 2002

❹ Phlem Loskott and One Smoking Mono — 8b S2
From the twin-barrel pockets on *Loskot and Two Smoking Barrels*, move left on small holds into *Right Here, Right Now*.
FA. Ethan Pringle 2019

❺ Loskot and Two Smoking Barrels — 8a+ S2
One of the most energetic deep water solos in Spain to date. Features a f7C+ boulder problem at 12m, which is essentially a gigantic dyno for a twin-barrel pocket. You have been warned!
FA. Klem Loskot 10.2001

❻ Ejector Seat — 7c S1
Another great route. Fire up the steep, pocketed face to a crux move for a tufa pinch, then swing right to easier ground.
Photo cover and p.5.
FA. Neil Gresham 10.2001

❼ In the Night, Every Cat is Black — 7c+ S1
Immaculate climbing up the brown streaks; with blind moves making things tricky. Save some energy for the move into the faint groove and finish more easily there after. *Photo p.39.*
FA. Klem Loskot 10.2001

❽ Hair Bear — 7c+ S1
The horrendously steep wall leftwards from the *Afroman* cave, to arrive at a complex sequence getting past a vertical slot. Thereafter trend right to enter the easier niche.
FA. Ken Palmer 10.2001

❾ Ronatron — 7b+ S1
A very steep line. From *Afroman*, swing left and take the bulging wall on hidden pockets. The top section eases considerably.
FA. Miquel Riera 2001

❿ Afroman — 7b S1
One of Diablo's most sort after climbs. Incredibly steep climbing leads out of the cave on large pockets then it gets tricky as the angle eases a little. Eventually slap to gain a horizontal seam and traverse left to gain the niche and a much-needed rest. Continue more easily leftwards and up to victory! *Photo p.9.*
FA. Tim Emmett 10.2001

Cova del Diablo - The Lobster Area — Porto Cristo — 37

Cova del Diablo - The Lobster Area

The central section of this fantastic wall gives more mega-quality routes and more buckets. As with the left side, timing your visit to coincide with dry rock can pay dividends. The small tides are inconsequential but pay close attention to the sea state and avoid choppy seas.

Approach - Central section (map and overview p.32) - The abseil to the base of *The Lobster* requires a swing and clip (into threads), which allows you to reach routes from *The Lobster* through to *In the Night all Cats are Black*. *Hair Bear* through to *Calamares*, are accessed via the *Easy Way Down* and traversing round via the line of *Superwoman* to the cave.

Exit - Take care with your exit here. Use the rope ladders below the two caves or the main exit point under the *Easy Way Down*.

⓫ Afroman - Direct Finish .... 7b+ *S1*
As for *Afroman* but from the horizontal break, pull up via a shallow pocket for the right hand, the make a long reach to deeper pockets above.

⓬ Whiplash 7c *S1*
A steep and technical route starting at the right side of the cave and finishing up *Calamares*. Hard to flash.
FA. Neil Gresham 10.2001

⓭ Calamares 6c *S1*
Follow the line of *Superwoman* to the point where you start to move around into the cave (or alternatively start from the cave and traverse right). Launch directly upwards through a steep pocketed wall - good holds throughout but tricky in parts. Things then begin to ease, but not before an exciting but relatively easy short layback halfway up. Easier climbing thereafter.
FA. Neil Gresham 10.2001

⓮ Dogging Romp .... 6a+ *S0*
Steep and juggy, and at an amenable grade - a brilliant introduction to the crag. From the easy way down, head leftwards up an enticing diagonal feature. When the moves start to get tricky, take a look up, grasp big jugs, and finish straight up over the bulging roof.
FA. Mike Robertson 10.2001

⓯ Superwoman .... 7a+ *S0*
100m+. Stunning climbing, weaving across the entire face of Diablo. This mini-expedition ventures to half height in places, and could perhaps be better described as a girdle, with the preferred direction seemingly right to left (looking in). Because it is such a lengthy outing, it naturally falls into four sections, with three excellent rests en-route.
1) 6b. Climb leftwards from the easy way down, to gain the rest in the *Afroman* start cave.
2) 7a+. The crux pitch. Traverse leftwards and down out of the cave (keeping low) onto a block feature. Make desperate moves off it to gain easier ground. Alternatively, embark on a lengthy and sustained traverse left out of the cave across the wall and then down climb to easier ground to rest under the start of *The Lobster*.
3) 7a. Climb leftwards, gaining more and more height, to reach a cave (rest). Climb left on big holds over very steep and pumpy ground to reach the big recess at the finish of *Iguanadon*.
4) 6b+. The final pitch is juggy and nicely sustained, heading across the steep wall to gain easier ground left of *The Italian Job*. Your choice now is to either finish for that route, or up the easier but less safe wall to the left. You can traverse all the way out, to reach the conglomerate bowl cave to the south.
FA. Ken Palmer, Grant Farquhar, Mike Robertson 10.2001

⓰ Easy Way Down 4a *S2*
For the tick-box obsessed. Climb up the easy way down.
FA. Mike Robertson 10.2001

⓱ First Impressions 6a *S1*
The colourful prow just to the right of the easy way down.
FA. Mike Robertson 10.2001

Cova del Diablo - White Noise Area

At this end of the crag you will find the usual buckets and pockets, but with a sudden change in angle - it's a perfect place to get acquainted with Diablo with friendly grades to match.

Approach - Right (map and overview p.32) - The final routes are easily reached using the *Easy Way Down* and or the traverse of *White Noise*.

Exit - Climb here only when the sea is calm and make sure that you can exit at the boulder beach, or rig the base of *Easy Way Down* with a rope.

❶ The Last Slice............ 6a+ S2
The prow that *Slice of Heaven* skirts around.
FA. Jamie Sparkes 2017

❷ Slice of Heaven......... 5a S1
In a world with very few really brilliant easy deep water solos, this one stands high! Climb the left side of the cave any way you see fit and at the prow, make some blind moves right to reach a juggy groove. Climb this to an exciting finish.
FA. Mike Robertson 10.2001

Lots of sun — 2 min

❸ Eternal Flame.............. 5c S1
All the pockets of the main cove, but on vertical territory. From the right side of the cave, climb the wall moving slightly leftwards at the top.
FA. Mike Robertson 10.2001

❹ Felix...................... 5c S1
A nice climb starting just left of *Bonobo*. Climb up and left to a short arete at the top of the crag.
FA. James Cole 9.2006

❺ Bonobo.................... 5c S2
Follow *White Noise* to a bit of a rest on a slab underneath a curling, brown groovy feature. Take this feature using jugs on its steeper right rib.
FA. Mike Robertson 10.2001

❻ Retronobo................. 5c S1
Follow the path of *White Noise* left to the smooth slab. Climb the groove to the right of this on good holds and the prow above.
FA. Mike Robertson 10.2001

❼ White Noise.......... 5c S0
60m+. Wonderful climbing across clean rock with numerous pockets and the odd tricky move. Normally done from right to left, finishing at the cave at the bottom of the easy way down. It's a good way to make your way into the cove. Continue (if you can) into *Superwoman* for the ultimate tick!
FA. Mike Robertson 10.2001

← Water exit

Landing platform swim out

An unknown climber concentrating hard on *In the Night, Every Cat is Black* (7c+) - *p.36* - at Cova del Diablo, Porto Cristo. Photo: Mike Hutton

Porto Cristo — Tower of Falcons

Tower of Falcons

The Tower of Falcons is on the opposite side of Porto Cristo town to Cova del Diablo. Use the large cliff-top tower to locate the area. It is quite an intimidating place with a selection of mostly hard climbs.

Approach (map p.32) - Drive south out of Porto Cristo, up the hill from the small bridge, and take the forth exit of the roundabout signed 'Torre dels Falcons'. Drive down here to park at the tower. More parking is just southwest at the end of Carrer Bitacola. *Shrek* is about 250m south of the tower at the bottom of an easy way down. The start to *Morning Glory* is slightly northeast, where you can descend to a large ledge. *La Hostia* and *Toni* are best reached via a rope-assisted descent to the right of *Forat*. *Sa Valenta* needs a dry-bag swim to a ledge in the cave.

Exits - Most of the crag is undercut, so for *Shrek, Feist Queen* and *Public Enema,* use a pre-placed rope exit. For *Morning Glory* swim back to the ledge. Routes near *La Hostia* require a swim into the cave to exit. *Sa Valenta* is just a swim back to the ledge under the route. **Always install a rope for exiting the water where you can.**

❶ Shrek 6a S0
180m. A relatively easy left-to-right traverse out of the bay and onto the main wall. Finish up a corner flake on the main face.
FA. Gav Symonds 10.2001

❷ Feist Queen 6c S3
A serious solo - only 2m of water! Continue traversing past the end of *Shrek* and across a caved section to climb the centre of the bulging wall to the right. The crux is near the top.
FA. Mike Robertson 10.2001

❸ Public Enema No.1 ...... 6b S2
From halfway up *Feist Queen,* escape right and up a groove for an easier finish. Keep an eye on the water depth below.
FA. Grant Farquhar 10.2001

❹ Shrek Extension ..... 6c+ S0
Traverse 15m beyond the start of *Feist Queen,* across the face. Jump off and swim back, or solo out above - not a DWS.
FA. Ken Palmer 10.2001

The next set of routes are in the big cave.

❺ Sa Valenta 6c S3
Climb the block to the inner cave. Watch the underwater ledge and don't fall! Reverse it.
FA. Miguel Riera 2006

❻ La Hostia .... 8a+ S3
A fantastic line which was originally approached from *Sa Valenta* to the huge stalactite. Alternatively, approach from the right (using a pre-placed rope ladder) and move left to the same stalactite. From there, move across the huge roof to the lip then go up and left to the headwall and tackle this if you still have anything left.
FA. Chris Sharma 2006

Tower of Falcons Porto Cristo 41

7 Toni....................... 7c+ *S1*
Climb the right-hand side of the cave mouth to the roof.
Continue up and slightly rightwards to the top.
FA. Toni Lamprecht 2006

8 Forat....................... 7c *S1*
From the cave where *Morning Glory* finishes, tackle the bulging
wall above to a ledge. The upper section needs care.
FA. Toni Lamprecht 2006

9 Red Tide........ 8a *S2*
The red face to the right of *Forat*.
FA. Ethan Pringle 2007

10 Hard Way Down .... 7a+ *S2*
Hard as a down-climb.

11 Morning Glory... 7a+ *S1*
100m. From the large platform, traverse left towards the cave.
The hard bit comes near the end as you make a rising traverse
up to a small cave at one-third height. Jump from here.
FA. Mike Robertson 10.2001

To the right of the main crag is a short headland.

12 You Wanner Intro 5a *S1*
A left-to-right traverse finishing up a slab.
FA. John Bull 5.5.2008

13 You Wanner Outro 6a *S2*
Down climb a corner (3) located on the nose of the headland
to sea level. Traverse left and eventually diagonally upwards to
ledges to finish.
FA. John Bull 5.5.2008

Porto Cristo Novo

Grade Spread - 1 5 1 1

The spectacular cave of Porto Cristo Novo was first discovered by Ken Palmer and Adam Wainwright in 2002 and is Mallorca's equivalent to the Grande Grotta in Kalymnos with its giant stalactites hanging from the roof of the cave. This venue is a serious undertaking requiring a boat to get to the routes and good calm conditions to get there. The top of the crag is overgrown so top-outs need a bit of planning. Another issue is that tourist boats drive into the cave in the summer months, which makes climbing on the stalactites potentially dangerous if the boat is not aware enough. Outside school and public holidays - October onwards - this is less of a problem.

Approach
From Porto Cristo, follow signs to Porto Colom (Ma-4014) for about 1km to the first roundabout and take the third exit signed Cala Magrana. Drive south towards the coast and take the second turning on the right followed by the first left onto Paseo de la Infanta Carlota. Drive for about 450m and park. Walk south and locate the pedestrian crossing which is in front of the small supermarket. A path opposite leads to the beach. From here, head out across the left-hand side of the bay along the short cliff until you reach a small area where it is possible to enter the water. Use your boat to paddle around to the left until you reach the cave.

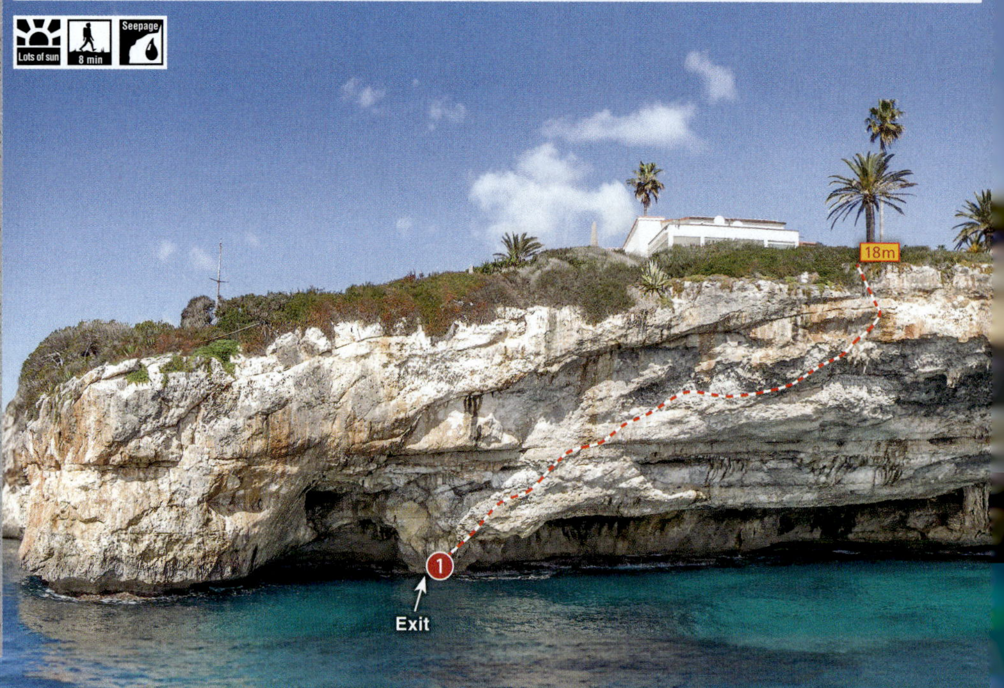

Porto Cristo Novo 43

1 Up the Anty .... 6c+ *S1*
Start at the left-hand side of the main cave and climb diagonally right over some steep terrain to the featured upper wall.
FA. Cas Ladha 9.2007

2 He Who Dares Rodders .. 7b *S1*
Start on the right-hand side of the cave. Traverse left around the arete and into the cave to eventually gain some huge black stalactites. Pull around on undercuts to finish direct on the crimpy headwall... which may well see you in the drink.
FA. Neil Gresham 7.2002

3 Geordie Racer 7a *S1*
Climb the right side of the arete to just above the lip of the cave. Swing left and finish to the right of *He Who Dares Rodders*.
FA. Ged Desforges 9.2007

4 The Banana Man Project . ? *S2*
A powerful and scary roof climb. Climb *Geordie Racer* to half height then traverse left into the cave to reach a black hole. Climb the roof out to the highest point of the cave on jugs. Pull onto the headwall on good pockets to a key double pocket above the lip - 7c to this point. The moves above on small crimps for the final 2m have yet to see an ascent.
FA. (to the double pocket) Bernard Boch 2.8.2018

The wall to the right (looking in) of the cave has a few routes. They can be approached either from the exit on the right of the cave and traversing the route *Retro Cruiser*, or by an exit point some distance to the right (boat required).

5 Retro Cruiser 6c *S0*
From the exit point on the left side of the wall, traverse the slab to the bulge. Use a pocket to climb over the bulge and gain the big flake. Finish direct from here.
FA. Cas Ladha 9.2007

6 My Name is Jackie 7a *S0*
A slight extension to *Baby Loader* which links into *Retro Cruiser*.
FA. Ged Desforges 9.2007

7 Baby Loader .... 6b+ *S0*
From the ledge, move left and down, to swing left to the right of the two grooves. Climb up this then move right to a large pocket and finish direct.
FA. Ged Desforges 9.2007

8 Esperanza 5a *S0*
The easy crack.
FA. Ged Desforges 9.2007

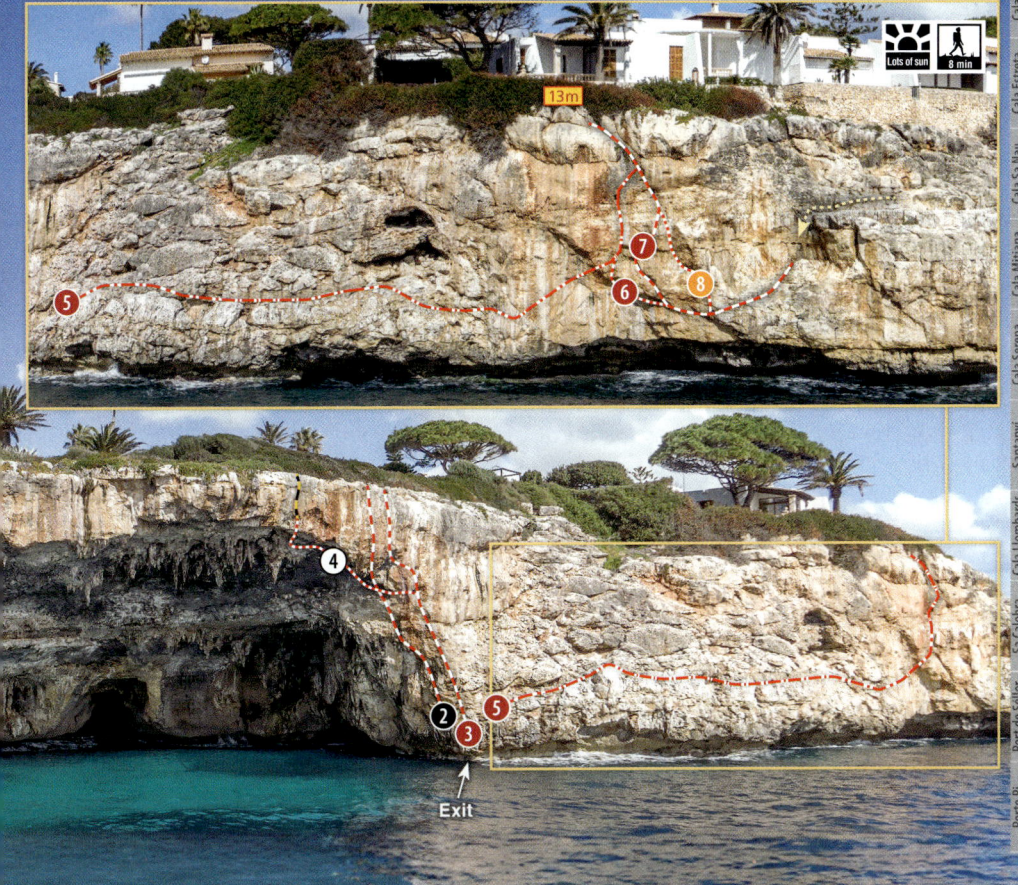

Cala Barques

Grade Spread - 7 27 23 9

Cala Barques (also known as Cala Varques) is one of the more inviting and less intimidating venues for DWS on Mallorca and has become very popular. It is a beautiful and relaxing spot with a lovely (but busy) beach near by. The routes are not too high in the main areas and most are S0.

One of the main areas to explore is the Cova Area - a 14m high cave with a row of stalactites at its centre - home to many a good climb without risking too much of a fall. Further out towards the open water is a bay where the twin caves of *Metrosexual* and *Snatch* are located which offer the most popular climbing, conveniently supplied with a lovely view platform opposite. The *Snatch* cave can also be accessed from a giant grotto cave set back from the cliff edge.

A bit further over on the same headland is the Tarantino Cave, the largest cliff in Barques, which has some of the most challenging routes on the island. Further round is the impressive Muscles Cave which has only one route so far.

Access

Cala Barques has become a victim of its own success becoming very popular, not only with climbers, but also the general public enjoying its idyllic sandy beaches and bays. The problems this created with car parking has resulted in the closure of the original unpaved road leading down to the bay. The current approaches are slightly longer but have alleviated the problems.

Conditions

The Barques area enjoys good conditions, although the usual rules apply with steep rock and shade - a dry, cool day will give you your best chance. Pay attention to the sea state, and sort out your water exits.

Angie Scarth-Johnson deploying strong head game on *Strangers in Paradise* (7b+) - *p.54* - at the Snatch Area of Cala Barques. Photo: Matty Hong

Cala Barques

GPS 39.517254, 3.308600

Porto Cristo Novo p.42

Cala Mendia

Cala Romantica

Ma-4014

Alternative parking

Cala Barques

1km N

Cala Barques beach (also called Cala Varques)

Cova Area
p.48

Cala Barques

Approach
The best approach is from the large Estany d'en Mas beach side car park in Cala Romantica. On the opposite side of the beach to the car park a well-worn path heads up the wooded hillside. Take the right branches of the path and, after a short distance, it leaves the woods onto flat open ground. Continue to where the path crosses a wider path and go left to the edge of the cliff. Follow the path to Cala Falco and then up onto the plateau above Tarantino/Muscle Cave. Follow the edge of the cliff to a massive arch and then continue to a small inlet where the Metrosexual and Snatch Areas are. The Cova Area is a short walk way over the promontory where the actual beach of Cala Barques can be seen. Good shoes are a must for this approach.

The old approach down a road leading towards the beach is now closed, although you can use an alternative parking spot on a bend on the main road and walk in this way - most visiting the beach choose this option.

Cala Barques — Cova Area

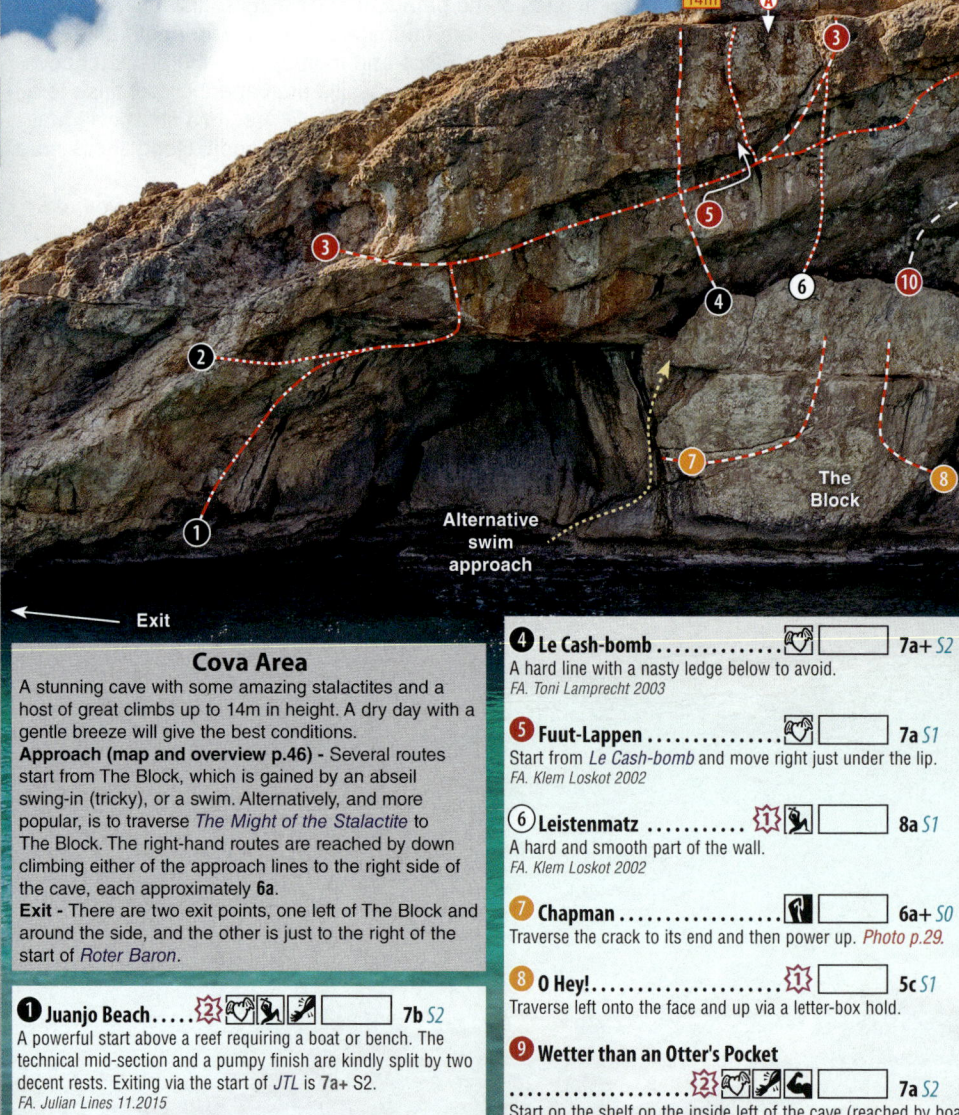

Cova Area

A stunning cave with some amazing stalactites and a host of great climbs up to 14m in height. A dry day with a gentle breeze will give the best conditions.
Approach (map and overview p.46) - Several routes start from The Block, which is gained by an abseil swing-in (tricky), or a swim. Alternatively, and more popular, is to traverse *The Might of the Stalactite* to The Block. The right-hand routes are reached by down climbing either of the approach lines to the right side of the cave, each approximately **6a**.
Exit - There are two exit points, one left of The Block and around the side, and the other is just to the right of the start of *Roter Baron*.

❶ Juanjo Beach 7b S2
A powerful start above a reef requiring a boat or bench. The technical mid-section and a pumpy finish are kindly split by two decent rests. Exiting via the start of *JTL* is 7a+ S2.
FA. Julian Lines 11.2015

❷ Juanjo Beach - Left-hand Start 7b S1
A dryer and slightly easier start to the original.
FA. Julian Lines 11.2015

❸ JTL .... 6c+ S2
Traverse right keeping an eye for the boulder below at the start. Finish by climbing into the final section of *Leistenmatz*.
FA. Julian Lines 9.2002

❹ Le Cash-bomb .... 7a+ S2
A hard line with a nasty ledge below to avoid.
FA. Toni Lamprecht 2003

❺ Fuut-Lappen 7a S1
Start from *Le Cash-bomb* and move right just under the lip.
FA. Klem Loskot 2002

❻ Leistenmatz 8a S1
A hard and smooth part of the wall.
FA. Klem Loskot 2002

❼ Chapman .... 6a+ S0
Traverse the crack to its end and then power up. *Photo p.29*.

❽ O Hey! 5c S1
Traverse left onto the face and up via a letter-box hold.

❾ Wetter than an Otter's Pocket 7a S2
Start on the shelf on the inside left of the cave (reached by boat or dry-bag swim). Climb the steep prow on tufa side-pulls to a shelf. Step left onto the stalactites (boulder below) and make your way through the stalactites to a rest. Move up on pockets to reach *The Might of the Stalactite* and reverse this to the start.
FA. Julian Lines 11.2015

❿ Oachikas 7a S0
A popular line. From The Block, launch straight into the roof on good holds which lead to the upper wall where the tricky bit is.
FA. Klem Loskot 2002

Cova Area — Cala Barques

⓫ Sixty's Silver Surfer 7a *S1*
Link *Oachikas* into *Erection*.
FA. Klem Loskot 2002

⓬ Drop Shadow Diseases .... 6c+ *S0*
A popular link-up. Start as for *Oachikas* and follow the natural line rightwards to join the top section of *Transversal*.
FA. Miquel Riera 2003

⓭ Erection 7b *S0*
Start from The Block and make your way rightwards over the roof which leads to easier face climbing above.
FA. Klem Loskot 2002

⓮ The Might of the Stalactite ... 6c+ *S0*
A right-to-left traverse over the lip of the cave. A must-do!
Photo p.2.
FA. Klem Loskot 2002

To reach the next routes, follow The Might of the Stalactite to the starting points or start them from The Block.

⓯ Double Penetration .... 7b+ *S0*
An alternative start to *Erection* from the largest stalactite here.
FA. Toni Lamprecht 2003

⓰ Transversal 7a *S0*
Independent and bold. Everyone is impressed with this one!
FA. Werner Gamsjager 2002

⓱ Supermarket Fantasy ... 7b *S0*
Climb to the roof on moderate holds. Navigate the roof to gain the vertical wall above finishing on numerous small edges.
FA. Toni Lamprecht 2003

⓲ Big XXL 7a *S0*
A mega classic! Start from The Block and reverse *The Might of the Stalactite* until you begin to naturally elevate towards a small cave in the wall. Rest here before tackling the finale, which involves a pull over the roof to a good pocket, followed by a rising traverse to join *Roter Baron* at a large bucket hold.
FA. Toni Lamprecht 2002

Down climb to reach the start of the next three routes.

⓳ Granaten-Einstieg ...... 7a+ *S0*
Often greasy at the start and not fully independent. Cutting out right onto *Big XXL* reduces the grade to **7a**.
FA. Marti Weinlander 2003

⓴ Granaten Woman .... 7b+ *S0*
Start as for *Granaten-Einstieg* and, when you join the line of *The Might of the Stalactite*, head up and left to traverse the roof to a junction with *Erection*. From here, power upwards to gain the final moves of *Oachikas*.
FA. Toni Lamprecht 2003

㉑ Roter Baron 6c *S0*
A parallel line to *Granaten-Einstiez*. The upper wall is much easier. Previously known as *Mecca*.
FA. Toni Lamprecht 2002 and previously known as Mecca.

㉒ Genoveses 6b *S0*
The line just left of the Darth Vader's helmet feature. Sometimes used as an alternative finish to *The Barques Traverse*.
FA. Miquel Riera 2003

Cala Barques — Cova Area

23 Cova Descent — 6a+ S0
The common approach descent is a decent climb in its own right.

24 Ralph Kaiser's Neue Kleider — 6c S1
Climb the vague flake and pockets via some committing moves to gain the undercuts under the roof. Continue over with difficulty using the flake out right.
FA. Martin Weinlander 2003

25 She — 6c+ S1
Thin and technical climbing up the blank looking face right of *Ralph Kaiser's Neue Kleider*.
FA. Martin Weinlander 2004

26 Trekin' Herd — 6a S1
The crack-line, moving left at the top.
FA. Dan Swygart 2018

27 Goldene Nase — 7b S2
Slabby climbing leads to a technical steep section above. Not often done due to the landing.
FA. Toni Lamprecht 2003

28 Kurt Husser — 7b+ S1
Follow *Goldie Hawn* to the final bulge and move left onto the finish of *Goldene Nase*.
FA. Toni Lamprecht 2003

29 Goldie Hawn — 7b+ S1
An increasingly popular line. Start at the left side of an in-cut and head direct up the groove and onto the upper face. A hard technical move above sees most people back in the water.
FA. Toni Lamprecht 2003

30 Tower of Power — 7a S0
Not very popular because of the quality of *Golden Shower*.
FA. Toni Lamprecht 2003

31 Golden Shower — 7a S0
This is the most popular line on this section of the cliff. Start to the left and move into the start via a juggy rail (or direct to the same point). The rest is tricky, but very entertaining.
Photo opposite.
FA. Klem Loskot 2002

32 Klem Beach — 6b+ S2
A wealth of sloping pockets leads the way up this wall. Take care of the boulder underneath.

33 The Barques Traverse — 6b S2
80m+. A long and fairly easy right-to-left traverse (starting 40m to the right of the big crack (see topo) via an easy way down), which eventually tackles the final section of *Big XXL*. There are one or two spots to watch out for, with protruding ledges above and below the water. Water exits can be found along the way.
FA. Daimon Beail 2005

An unknown climber on *Golden Shower* (7a) - *opposite* - in the Cova Area at Cala Barques. This superb testpiece should be on the top of your wish list, if you are climbing or aiming at that grade. Photo: Mike Hutton

Cala Barques — Metrosexual Area

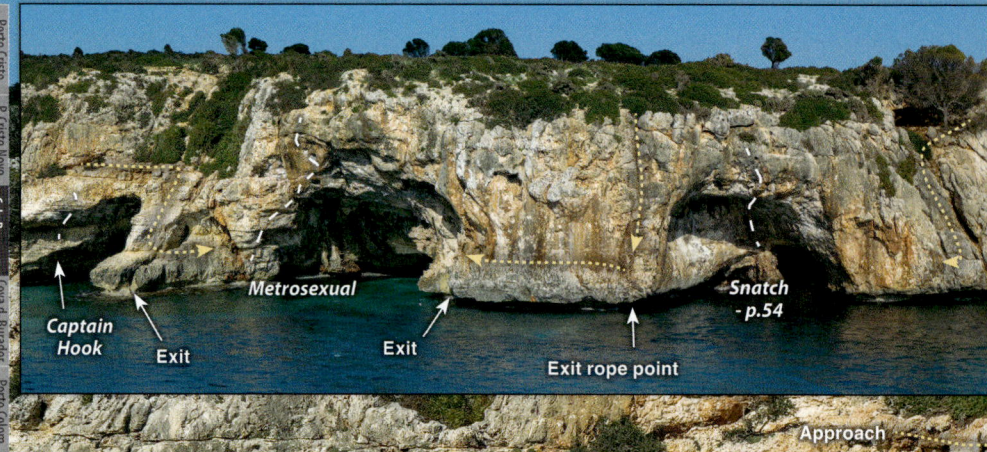

Metrosexual Area

The Metrosexual Area is arguably the most popular DWS spot in Mallorca. Its height of 12m with cruxes usually way below this mean that falls are less scary. Most routes are S0 and have easy exits if set up correctly. The crag is generally sheltered but, like all cave climbs, can be greasy. However, any dry, sunny day should give you plenty to do. Avoid if there is a swell since the area can turn into a major wave machine.

❶ Left Cave Traverse 6b S0
A short but interesting warm-up line on the side of the small cave which is just left of the Metrosexual cave. The line is best finished by reversing or swimming back to the exit point.

❷ Left Cave Traverse - Flake Finish
.... 6a S1
Exiting via the flake at the halfway mark reduces the grade and keeps you dry.

❸ Captain Hook 6c S2
Near the end of the *Left Cave Traverse*, find the undercut in the roof and head direct to finish via a white dish. The first few moves are still above the ledge.
FA. Edward Teale 30.9.2017

❹ El Door 7a S1
A right-to-left circumnavigation of the cave. Mind the boulder at the start. The hard climbing is on the left wall low down along the rail until the lip is reached. Continue left until its possible to exit. Either reverse the *Left Cave Traverse* or finish up the flake. Also done as a left-to-right continuation of *Left Cave Traverse*.
FA. Jamie Sparkes, Fran Hammond 26.9.2017

Metrosexual Area **Cala Barques** 53

Approach (map and overview p.46) - The first mini cave is reached from the side though the exit to the main traverse climb is often into the sea. The main Metrosexual Area routes are easily reached from the half-height platform or the sea-level ledge down and to the left. The right side of the Metrosexual cave is reached by a down-climb (5c) between the two main caves.

❺ Bisexual **7a** S0
Start from the upper left platform and traverse right, dropping down onto a thin rail which leads to a pocket. Launch up and right to the top. Harder for the short.
FA. Miguel Riera, Alex Huber 2005

❻ Metrosexual .... **7a+** S2
Start low down (watching the ledges to the left and below the water) and climb your way up past the platform and onto the upper wall. Follow *Bisexual* until you can move left to a tough finish. Often started from the platform. Photo p.12 and p.18.
FA. Toni Lamprecht, Miguel Riera 2003

❼ Asexual .... **6b+** S0
The first part of *Metrosexual*, but moving left to finish at the ledge.

❽ Transexual **7b** S0
Traverse right from *Bisexual* across the upper wall and onto the final section of *Bandito*. Can also be started from the lower wall.
FA. Toni Lamprecht 2004

❾ Hot Chili **7b** S0
A direct finish to *Transexual* up the crack.
FA. Fer Zemelman 2015

❿ Pansexual **7a** S0
Climb *Transexual* to undercuts and continue right to finish.
FA. Remus Knowles 4.10.2024

⓫ Smash it in! **8a** S0
Start deep in the back of the cave (gained from the right-hand side) and cross the roof. Join the finish of *Bandito*.
FA. Stu Littlefair 3.9.2007.

⓬ Bandito **7c** S0
From the well-featured section on the right-hand ledge, make a hard move to gain a large hold (mind the starting ledge). Rail leftward on improving holds (rest on the left) then trend slightly back right to the final bulge.
FA. Toni Lamprecht 2003

⓭ Solecito **7c** S0
Start as for *Bandito* then head left on large holds to join and finish up *Metrosexual*.
FA. Toni Lamprecht 2003

⓮ Homosexual **7b** S2
A steep route on large holds at the right-hand side of the cave. The easier start is above the ledge so be careful.

Cala Barques — Snatch Area

Snatch Area

This cave is a terrific way either to fall off a lot or get very fit. It's full of grade 6s and 8s, and they're (almost) all at the magic grade of S0. It is very sheltered and usually dry if there is a bit of a breeze.

Approach (map and overview p.46) - To reach the left-hand routes, use the down-climb (5c). For the routes on the right, either traverse *Watch for the Jellies*, or use the Grotto's entry scramble. Easily down climb to the right of the cave to reach *Braune Gurken*.

Exit - Take care when exiting in the Grotto, as there are some deep holes dotted about underfoot.

Approach (5c)
Approach via the Grotto
10m
Approach
Exit in Grotto and Start to *Catch 22*
Install exit rope here

① Fortuna .... 6a+ S0
An super line up the left side of the cave. Head up the crack and make some blind and tricky moves up and left.
FA. Miquel Riera 2003

② Hercules 6c S0
Start as for *Fortuna*, but head right from a thread, then continue up into the roof. Make some big swings on huge holds across the lip before pulling up to the top. An amazing line for the grade.
FA. Toni Lamprecht, Udo Endres 2003

For the rest of the routes, approach via the Grotto.

③ Watch for the Jellies .... 6c+ S0
A tricky, central traverse that starts in the Grotto and traverses around and across the scoop.
FA. Andrew Chapman 2006

④ Catch 22 .... 6c+ S0
This little outing makes its way through a small hole found inside the Grotto and out onto the main wall, just under the *Watch for the Jellies* traverse. Tricky moves are then made to reach the cave arch start of *Strangers in Paradise*.
FA. Bob Hickish 9.2006

⑤ Snatch .... 8a+ S0
The first of three classics. It's unbelievably fingery and smooth.
FA. Klem Loskot 2002

⑥ Carlos Checa 8a S0
Follow *Snatch* and continue heading rightwards into the scoop.
FA. Toni Lamprecht 2003

⑦ Strangers in Paradise ... 7b+ S1
Swing across the entrance of the Grotto and onto the adjacent wall - spotter advised. Move rightwards until you reach a series of ledges and pockets which help you attain a mega-pinch. Hold on! Continue making tricky moves up and right to finish.
Photo p.44 and opposite.
FA. Toni Lamprecht 2002

⑧ Stranger than Paradise . 8a S0
Connect *Strangers in Paradise* to the upper part of *Snatch*.
FA. Toni Lamprecht 2006

⑨ The R-Rodler 7c S0
Climb up the brown streak on monos and small edges.
FA. Thomas Starke 2006

⑩ Braune Gurken .... 6a+ S0
An easier offering with smooth holds for your feet. Move left from the approach then climb up a short steep groove.
FA. Martin Weinlander 2003

Cala Barques

Adam Lincoln on the classic *Strangers in Paradise* (7b+) - *opposite* - at the Snatch Area of Cala Barques. Photo: Beail Collection

Cala Barques — Tarantino Cave

Tarantino Cave

This cave is full of big grades. It's also tall, at roughly 22m! The cave is exposed to the open sea, so take extra care here. A mildly choppy day will give best conditions.

Approach (map and overview p.46) - Abseil in, since down climbing is risky. Lots of natural threads can be found at the top to attach your rope. Climbing out is possible at about 6a but a shunt or ascender should be used for back-up.

Muscles Cave **Cala Barques**

1 Big Mama .... 8a+ S2
A long, powerful and scary undertaking, especially at the top. Start at the back of the cave and cross the massive roof to the upper wall. Trend up leftwards across another roof with some big stalactites. The shallow start gives the S2 solo grade.
FA. Chris Sharma 2004.

2 Mamasita 8a S2
The 'Little Mama'. From the water ledge, head up and diagonally left for a short rest before joining *Big Mama* briefly at the bulge. Move back right to climb the short roof and wall above. A stamina testpiece of the highest order!
FA. Tony Lamprecht 2005

3 Jackie Brown 8b S2
A stamina-intensive link-up of *Mamasita* and *Big Mama* including a short independent section.
FA. Toni Lamprecht 2006

4 O-Ren Ishii 8a S2
Start as for *Mamasita* but move up and right to join *Kill Bill 2*. Follow this to the top.
FA. Tony Lamprecht 2004

5 Kill Bill 2 .... 7c S2
The best known route here. Start from the fin at the lower right edge of the cave. Climb up to the overlap and a no-hands rest. Pull over then move out right and continue direct to the top.
FA. Tony Lamprecht 2003

6 Kill Bill 1 .... 7b S2
The sightly easier Kill Bill twin. Traverse left along the line of *Kill Bill 2* but pull directly up the face, trending rightwards to easier ground. Make sure you keep a cool head!
FA. Tony Lamprecht 2003

7 From Dusk 'til Dawn .. 7c S2
Follow *Kill Bill 2* past the no-hands rest and onto the upper wall. Pull out left to climb the face just right of the golden streak.
FA. Tony Lamprecht 2003

8 Raticida 6b S2
From the starting fin, climb the wall just to the left up a flat-looking wall. A bit more of an adventure line than a DWS.
FA. Tony Lamprecht, Julian Heidinger 2005

Muscles Cave
This hidden bay lies further around the headland from Tarantino Cave and has a significant line. The crag faces northeast, getting early morning sun which helps to dry it out a bit.
Approach (map and overview p.46) - Walk east from the Tarantino Cave and continue north a short way until the bay can be seen on your right. Scramble down and across the base of the cave to reach the prow.

9 The Muscles from Brussels 7a+ S3
A spectacular line - big, committing and with the crux at the top! Climb the right-hand side of the prow on tufas and stalactites to obtain a semi-rest in a shallow cave at about half height. Above this, move diagonally up and right to finish with a long move past an orange streak at the top of the wall. Topping out at roughly 22m (vertical height) and with only about 4m of water this is a very serious route and a fall from the top would be ill advised.
FA. Jacob Cook 1.10.2010. A pre-placed exit rope was used for the first ascent, although it was done without on the same day by Ian Cooper.

Cova des Burador

Grade Spread - 4 9 - -

Cova des Burador is a dramatic and high sea cliff north of Porto Colom. The area is quite limited and more suitable for the experienced deep water connoisseur looking for some adventure. There are a number of routes spread out across four sections. The long traverse called *Adventure Land* (6a+) connects the first three.

There is some shallow water so take care soloing outside the described areas here or if committing to the traverse *Adventure Land*. Although the cliff is high, the top-outs on many of the lines are relatively easy angled. Potential still exists for new routes.

Take a rope and some slings and krabs to assist with access in one or two spots. Make sure your exit points are set up or identified before setting out on any route here.

Approach

Follow the Ma-4010 to Porto Colom. At the main roundabout, turn left and follow the road roughly straight through a built-up area. As you exit, turn right along the harbour wall. Very quickly the road turns sharply right. At this point turn left and drive up a dirt track heading northeast. Follow this to a rocky bay by the sea known as the Cove of S'Algar and a vague path that can be seen heading up the rising cliff to your left. Park here and head through a gate and up the hill. Riviera is the first section of climbable cliff shortly after the cliff begins to increase in height.

GPS 39.428825 / 3.272193

Cova des Burador

Conditions
The cliff faces east and catches the morning sun. It is large and exposed to the elements and is less steep than other crags in the area, which all helps reduce condensation and means it generally stays dry.

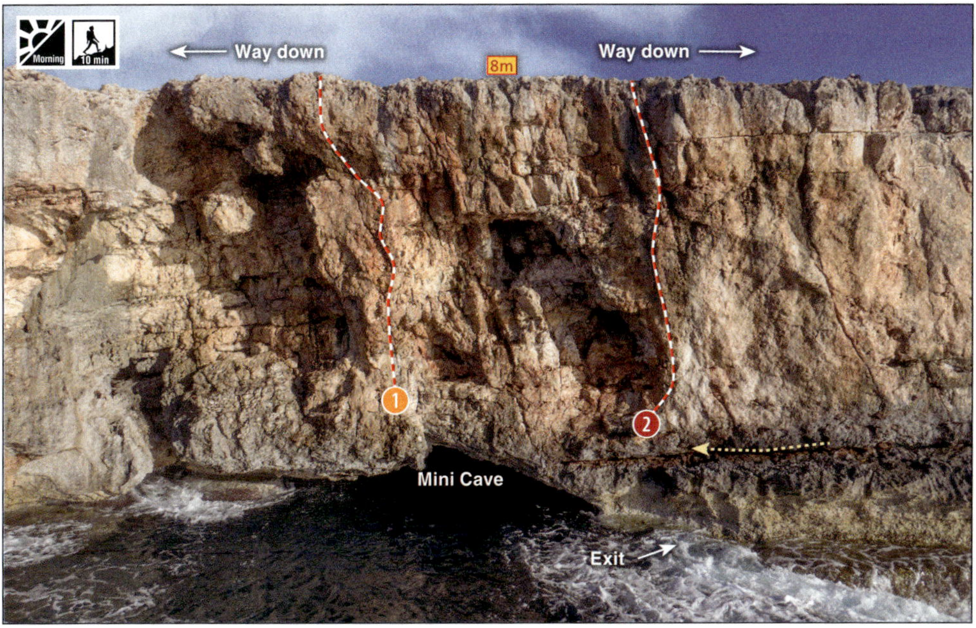

Riviera and Adventure Land
This is the first area you reach from the car park and the lines are easily accessed from the left (gear stash area) or the right-hand side.

❶ The Italian Riviera .... 6a+ *S0*
A gentle ride up the easy-angled face to tackle the roof above.
FA. Daimon Beail 3.10.2011

❷ Gluon 6b *S0*
Crimpy climbing up the slightly bulging face. Tricky to start.
FA. Bernard Exley 3.10.2011

❸ Adventure Land .... 6a+ *S3*
A long traverse of the crag that starts at the down-climb approach to *The Lion's Head*. Continue to just past the *One Tom* area. The exit is where it is no longer possible to solo above the water. You need to make an easy grade 3 solo (above a rocky platform) to meet the way down climb to the Dominion Wall area. There is also one easy section of climbing along your way where there is a significant ledge beneath you.
FA. Adam Brown, Tom Le Fanu, Daimon Beail 3.10.2011

Cova des Burador — Lion's Head and One Tom

Lion's Head
Approach (map and overview p.58) - Down climb to the left of the face and traverse rightwards.

① The Lion's Head 5c S0
Climb the line of jugs and pockets just to the right of the hanging arete. Move back left near the top.
FA. Adam Brown 3.10.2011

One Tom
Approach (map and overview p.58) - Descend a groove to the left of the area and easily walk rightwards. A knotted rope is needed for the top section of the descent.

② One Tom, One Cup ...... 6b+ S0
Start under a smooth leaning pillar where some deep finger-pockets mark the way. Launch up the pillar, avoiding the tempting cave to the right, until a technical move back left brings you to the finishing ledge. The top section is loose, so jump off or scramble down the easy way.
FA. Adam Brown 3.10.2011

③ In Memory Of 6b S1
Follow the crack to the roof and step left into a steep technical groove, eventually moving back right to finish up the crack.
FA. Bernard Exley 3.10.2011

Dominion Wall

Slightly further north up the coastline is the hidden Dominion Wall. This section offers the steepest ventures.
Approach (map and overview p.58) - As the cliff begins to decrease in height, keep an eye out for what looks to be an easy way down the cliff to a platform. Continue to scramble down about 4m to a sloping ledge, then continue down and round to the right (looking out) to an easy way down towards the sea. Traverse back right (looking in) around the corner (now at a lower level) towards the wall and the start of the routes. All lines are reached by traversing along *Techno Mancore!* which is fairly easy at the start. To get to the line *Dominion Wall* and beyond you have to do a 7a traverse or abseil in.
Conditions - The wall is made up of sandstone and limestone. It does not see much traffic so the top-outs are still a bit loose in places.

4 Techno Mancore! 7a S0
The main way to access all the lines on this wall. Watch out for those tricky bits near the end. Jump off to exit or try some of the lines above.
FA. Daimon Beail 25.9.2006

5 2D 3D .... 6b+ S0
Move diagonally up past a large horn (which you can sit on for a rest). The rest is highball climbing on large jugs.
FA. Adam Lincoln 25.9.2006

6 IMAX .... 6b+ S0
The original line on the wall. Follow *2D 3D* to the upper wall and make an airy traverse out over the lip of a bulging feature and onto the nose. The rest is easy.
FA. Daimon Beail 25.9.2006

7 The Camp Jogger .... 6c+ S0
Probably the best here. Traverse along *Techno Mancore!* to the bulging overhanging feature. Pumpy climbing on good holds takes you up to a mini-roof section and on to victory.
FA. Adam Lincoln 25.9.2006

The next few climbs require a traverse in along *Techno Mancore!* (7a) to reach the starts or alternatively an abseil in.

8 Dominion Wall 6b S1
An adventurous route and harder if traversing in along *Techno Mancore!* as originally done. From the platform, climb the left side of the face using a crack and hidden jugs. At the break, traverse right to reach an exit point up a shallow corner.
FA. Daimon Beail 25.9.2006

9 No Te Rindas 6b S1
Sustained climbing on vertical terrain. From the ledge at the end of the traverse *Techno Mancore!*, head diagonally rightwards to locate and follow a line of pockets all the way to the top.
FA. Frank Tetzel 5.8.2017

10 Maria mirame .... 6a+ S1
Continuing the traverse further right still, locate an under-cling and proceed to follow big holds diagonally to a groove and then head for the top. Keep a keen eye out for the underwater ledge when leaving the end of the traverse.
FA. Frank Tetzel 20.7.2018

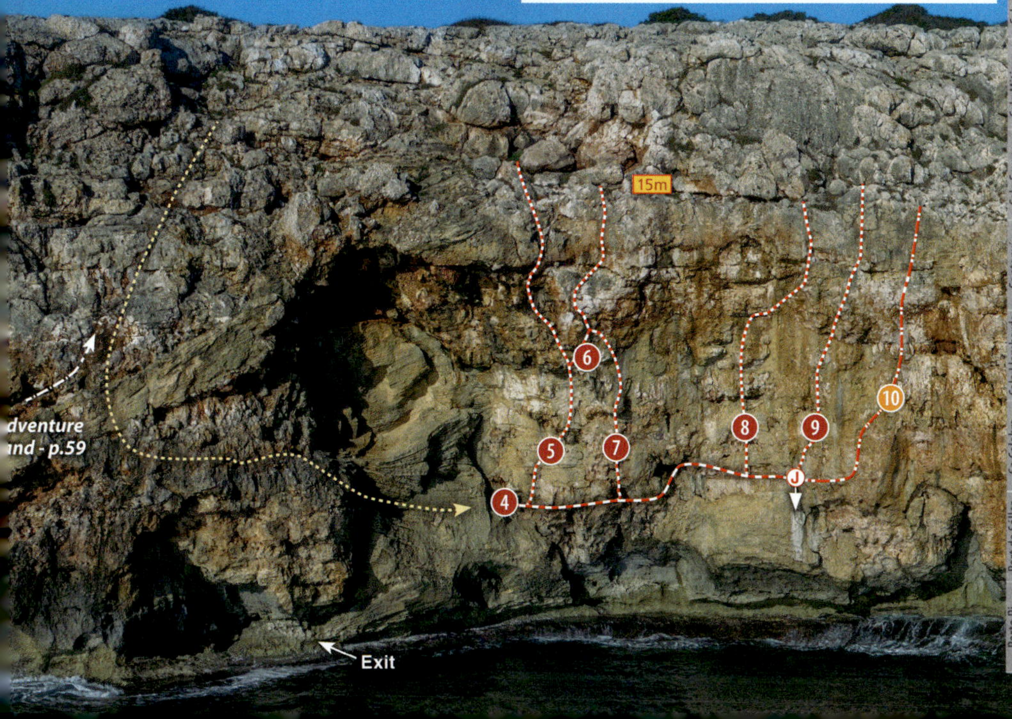

Porto Colom

Grade Spread - | - | 9 | 13 | -

Mike Robertson finishing *Drop Zone* (6c+) - *p.67* - the low traverse that is used to access many of the routes at Porto Colom. Photo: Mike Hutton

Hidden away underneath the Porto Colom lighthouse is this exciting venue, which is more suited to the roof-hungry boulderer who fancies a bit of deep water solo action. The classics of the crag are *Princess of Transilvania* and *I Live in a Cave*.

The lines on the lower section are short and relatively safe but the longer routes which top out are quite committing and generally don't see many ascents. Retreat is usually by jump, or reversing *I Live in a Cave*.

To the right side of the crag is a large platform where you can stow gear and hang out. It is also one of the few soloing venues were you can easily spectate without actually having to climb.

Conditions
The climbing is situated in a sheltered cove. The main part of the crag gets the sun in the middle of the day. As with all cave-style routes, some of the holds can get soapy but there is little seepage.

Porto Colom

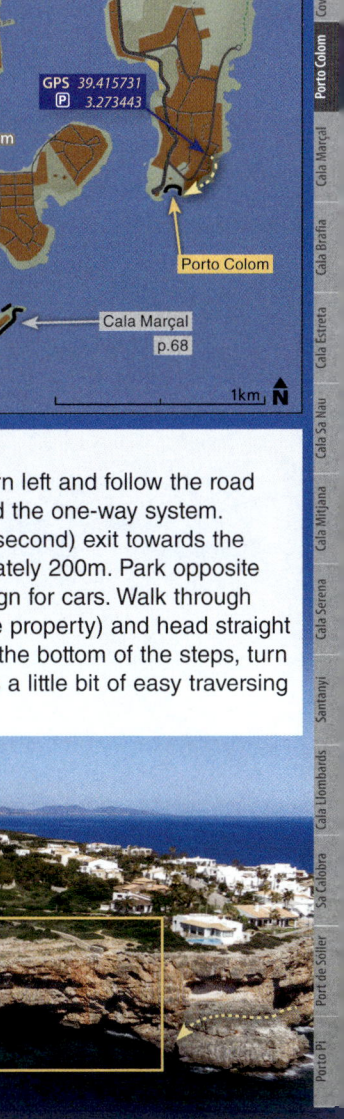

Approach
Follow the Ma-4010 to Porto Colom. At the main roundabout, turn left and follow the road round the bay and up towards the lighthouse. Branch left around the one-way system. Follow the road round to a small roundabout then take the left (second) exit towards the east cliff. Turn right at the junction and head south for approximately 200m. Park opposite an entrance with name 'Aldea Ibicenca N12' and a 'No Entry' sign for cars. Walk through this entrance (being discreet as this is an access road to private property) and head straight across to find some concrete steps leading down to the sea. At the bottom of the steps, turn right and walk about 200m along the rocky path (which requires a little bit of easy traversing in one or two spots) until you arrive at the crag.

Porto Colom

❶ Future Barny 7a S1
Tackle the overhanging arete to easier climbing above.
FA. Toni Lamprecht 2005

❷ Wenga Xavi 7b S1
Traverse in past the overhanging arete and climb the wall to its right. Pull through the overlap to an easier wall above.
FA. Toni Lamprecht 2005

❸ Chungulungu 7c S1
A hard start avoiding the ledge on the right. Higher up, trend right under the roof. Make some powerful moves to the cave and top out above, any way you like.
FA. Toni Lamprecht 2008

❹ No me puedo quejar .... 7a+ S1
Finish over a small roof. Alternatively move right to join the roof section of *Omprakash*. Both finishes are thoroughly enjoyable.
FA. Chris Sharma 2005

❺ Omprakash 7b S1
Difficult climbing up a blank corner to an increasingly steep wall above. Manoeuvre across the roof on good holds to the top.
FA. Chris Sharma 2005

The rest of the routes are accessed by doing Drop Zone.

❻ Rene Colo 7c S0
The more direct line to *Culo Superchulo*. Traverse out left and then up the flake. Where *Culo Superchulo* traverses right, continue to head diagonally up the face via some long moves before reaching the finishing ledge out right.
FA. Toni Lamprecht 2006.

❼ Culo Superchulo 7b S0
Move across the roof on small crimps and up the flake. Traverse right where things get blank and up to the vague ledge above.
FA. Toni Lamprecht 2005.

❽ Luciana 7b S1
A link-up between *Culo Superchulo* and the top half of *Omprakash*. Quite popular as an alternative mid-climb exit from the routes to its right.
FA. Miquel Riera 2005

Approach (map and overview p.63) - Routes are reached by *Drop Zone* apart from *Future Barny* to *Omprakash*, for which it is best to use a dry-bag to swim your gear to the other side.

Exit - Most people exit to the right of the crag onto the large platform. A rope is not generally needed, but is handy when the sea is rough or if you wish to set up an alternative exit point under the main cliff.

Nuria Valdes on *I live in a Cave* (6b+) - *p.66* - at Porto Colom. This is a fantastic little climb with all the fun over a short but challenging roof, low down and on big holds. Photo: Beail Collection

Porto Colom

⑨ The Rabbit is Dead ...... 7a+ S0
Climb the roof and head out over to the arete on the upper wall.
FA. Miquel Riera 2005

⑩ Mataconejos 7a S0
A direct version of *The Rabbit is Dead* which gains the upper wall using a crack-line which curves around to the left. Pull around the side of the roof and finish as for *The Rabbit is Dead*.
FA. Miquel Riera 2005

⑪ Princess of Transilvania.. 7a S0
Climb the stalactite rib on the roof using good pockets to the lip. Pull up on big holds to the stalactite formation and a possible rest. Move up and right to gain the upper face and layback your way up the crack to the ledge.
FA. Miquel Riera 2005

⑫ Tequila-men .... 7b+ S0
Big roof climbing to the upper wall.
FA. Bernhard Fiedler 2005

⑬ Baby Nate .... 6c+ S0
A short corner with some tricky roof climbing thrown in.
FA. Nate Gold 2005

⑭ I Live in a Cave .... 6b+ S0
A popular line. A short roof leads to a small deep cave - squirm in for a rest but avoid resting on the ledge to the right, this is off route. Continue up and right to a small roof and heave your way over onto the upper wall and to the ledge. *Photo p.65.*
FA. Miquel Riera 2005

⑮ S'atic .... 7a+ S2
Some people do this as a continuation to *The Rabbit is Dead*.
FA. Miquel Riera 2005

⑯ Niagara Will Fall .... 7a+ S2
A hero's medal awaits anyone trying this one! A possible continuation to *Princess of Transilvania*.
FA. Miquel Riera 2005

Approach (map and overview p.63) - All climbs are reached by traversing *Drop Zone*. *S'atic* to *No Man's Land* are reached from *I Live in a Cave* and traversing in either direction along the ledge to reach the desired line. Alternatively climb the lines directly below them.
Exit - Most people exit to the right of the crag onto the large platform. A rope is not generally needed, but is handy when the sea is rough or if you wish to set up an alternative exit point under the main cliff.

Lower Lip Traverse on Drop Zone, 7a

Exit

17 Cris Rabbit .... 1 ☐ 7a+ S2
Some serious highball action, and watch that ledge at the start.
FA. Miquel Riera 2005

18 No Man's Land .... 1 ☐ 7a+ S2
Originally done as an extension to *Princess of Transilvania* or possibly any of the lines to the right of this. Heart-pounding upper-wall action is best left to the brave and avoided on flat days.

The overhanging pillar nearest the platform on the near side incorporates the gateway to all the lines here via Drop Zone and a number of other challenging outings.

19 Mi llamo Chris .... ☐ 7a S1
The only route on this part of the wall which tops out. Climb the left side of the bulging face. Take care near the top, but the climbing is very much easier at this point.
FA. Miquel Riera 2005

20 Titan .... 1 ☐ 6c+ S0
Traverse onto the face and cross the white streak diagonally, then power your way up onto the small ledge. It is quite far to jump from the finishing point, so reverse a bit first.
FA. Toni Lamprecht 2005

21 Topspin .... 1 ☐ 7a S0
The right-hand variation to *Titan*. Again, this finishes rather high so a down-climb is recommended before jumping off.
FA. Toni Lamprecht 2005

22 Drop Zone .... 3 ☐ 6c+ S1
50m+. A popular traverse. Start on the right by moving around the arete and along a break-line to the platform under *I Live in a Cave*. Go left on the easiest line to a small shelf in the cave just past the start of *Rene Colo/Culo Superchulo*. Drop down low and move left into another small cave before a corner. Have a rest then blast out onto the rising break leading to the platform on the far side. The cave in the centre of the crag where *Tequila-men* starts can be traversed lower down - worth **7a**.
Photo p.62.
FA. Miquel Riera 2005

Porto Cristo
P. Cristo Novo
Cala Barques
Cova d. Burador
Porto Colom
Cala Marçal
Cala Braña
Cala Estreta
Cala Sa Nau
Cala Mitjana
Cala Serena
Santanyí
Cala Llombards
Sa Calobra
Port de Sóller
Porto Pi

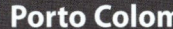

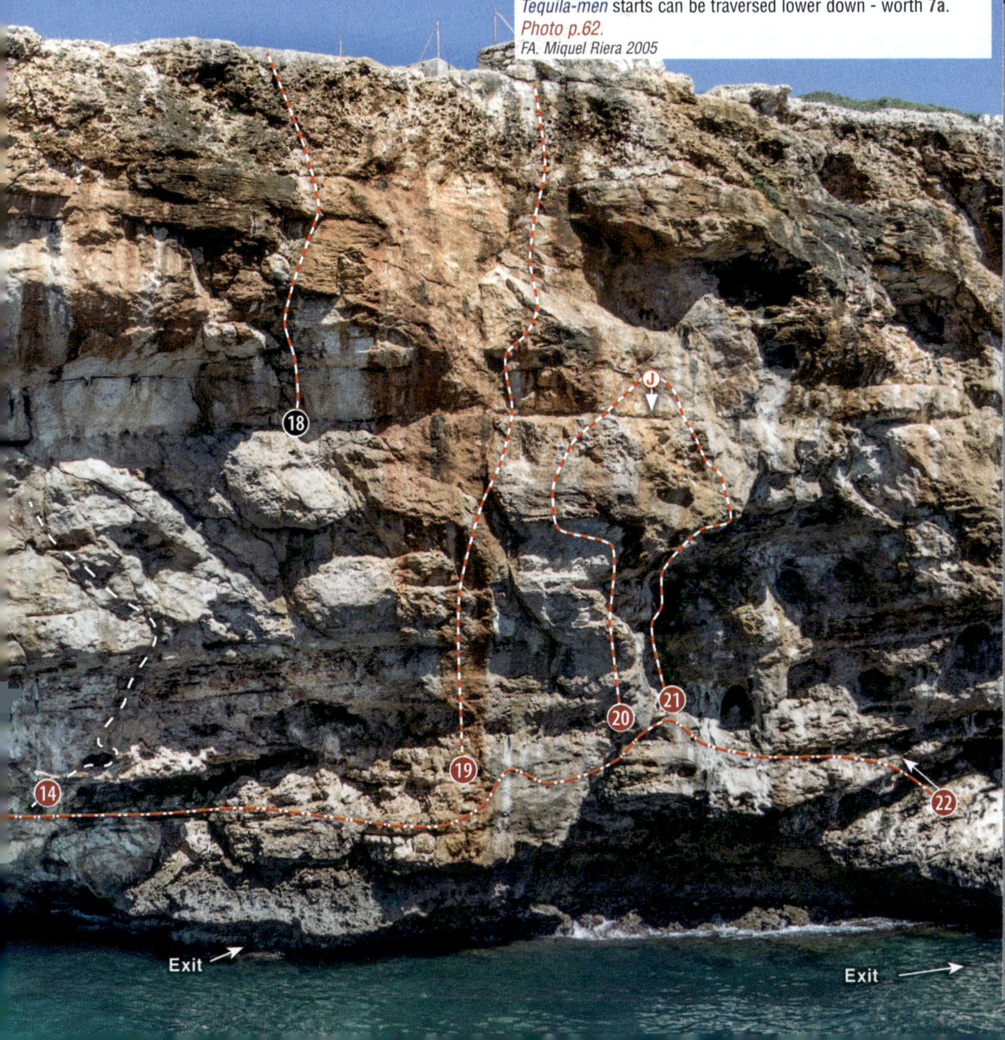

Cala Marçal

| Grade Spread | 2 | 17 | 7 | - | - |

Cala Marçal is one of the best roadside deep water soloing venues on the island. With a good selection of easy to mid-grade routes and a height more amenable to many, this makes for a perfect venue for those looking to progress their physical and mental calibre with regards to deep water solo climbing. There are four main sectors, all in relatively close proximity to each other. The Cala Wall offers a variety of traverses, whereas the more extensive cliff on the east side provides three more areas with the Main Cliff being the main attraction. The Eastern Walls and the Main Cliff creep up to about 16m high in places, but the climbing almost always eases off in the upper section.

Approach

Cala Marçal is just south of Porto Colom, some 20km south of Porto Cristo. From the Ma-4014 coastal road, turn eastwards along the Ma-4010 to Porto Colom or the next junction to the south which is also well signed. Then follow signs south to Cala Marçal and drop down to the beach. From here, swing around the bay and drive up the hill. Keep going around to the left (miss a dead-end left turn here) and continue until you reach a roundabout. Go straight ahead and park at the end of the road, where the main cliff is right beneath you.

Conditions

The Main Cliff is southeast facing, with shade later in the day. Early summer often finds it a bit greasy, but the vertical climbs here generally stay dry. The Cala Wall faces northeast, getting late afternoon sun only. Take the usual precautions when climbing close to a headland, and keep an eye open for possible currents.

Water Exits

Please note that exits here can prove tricky. It is possible to scramble out in one or two places, but you'll still be left with proper climbing to get back to the top of the crag. The best advice is to install a knotted rope or rope ladder utilising slings and crabs to fix it into place. A flotation of some kind (rubber ring is best) is also a very good idea.

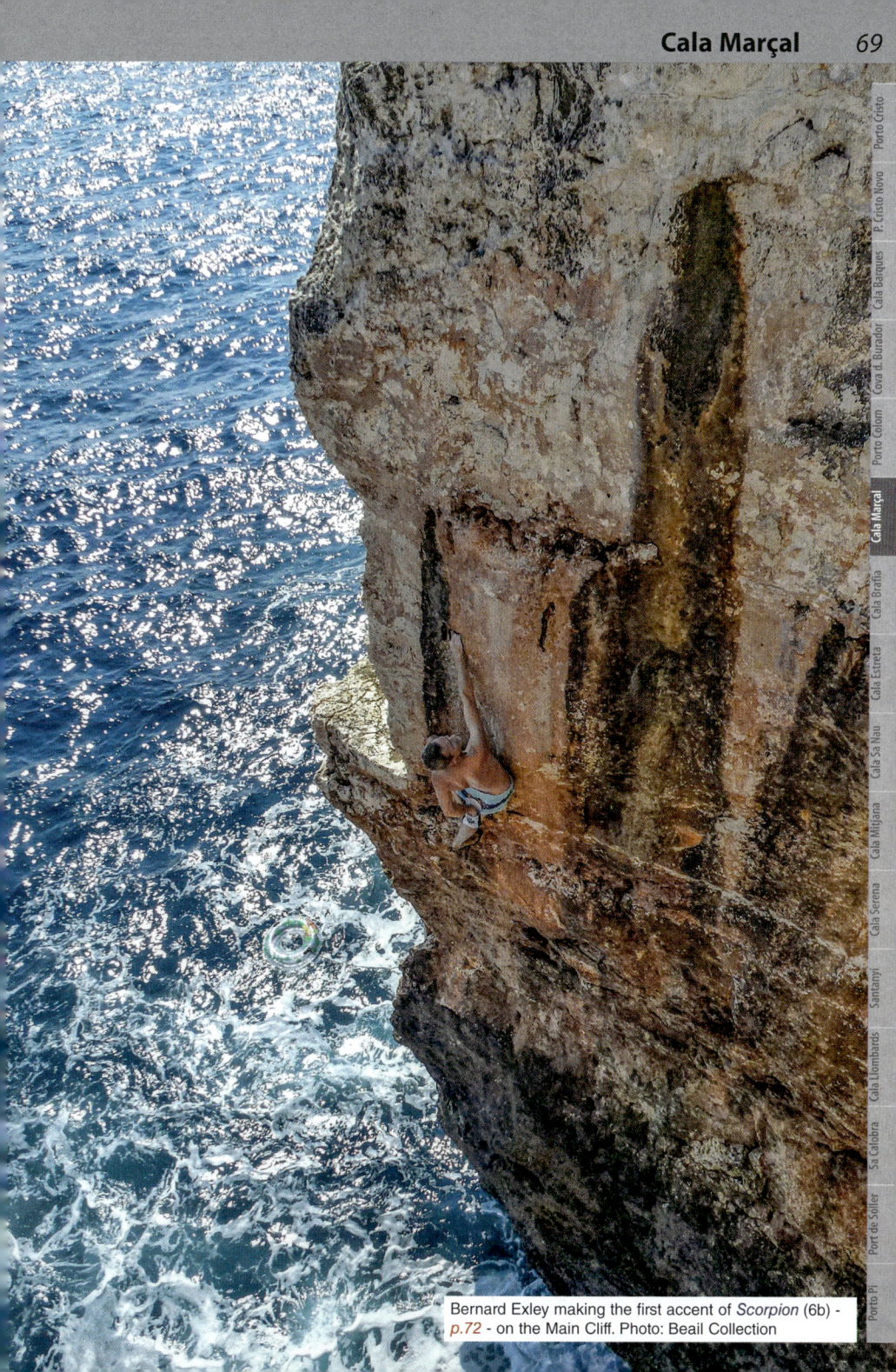

Bernard Exley making the first accent of *Scorpion* (6b) - *p.72* - on the Main Cliff. Photo: Beail Collection

Cala Marçal — Outlying Walls

Outlying Walls

The large section of cliff to the left of the Main Cliff has much potential and two recorded routes.

Approach (map and overview p.68) - The approach to *Cala What?* is roughly 80m south of the Main Cliff and the descent to *Rodio* is just to the left of the Main Cliff.

Exits - Numerous exits which are possible in calm seas, though ensure you have a rope set up and an inflatable somewhere along the way.

❶ Cala What? 6a S0
The steep right-hand side of the cave which is approached by traversing the inner cave from the left side.
FA. Bernard Exley 14.10.2012

❷ Rodio 6b S2
Drop down to the left side of the main crag to gain a nice right-to-left traverse. It has a low-level roof near its end (watch the water level here) then head up the arete above.
FA. Daimon Beail 2.10.2011. FA. (Final section) John Bull 5.2008

Andrew Chapman moving left on the upper half of *The Fat Crab* (6a+) - *p.72* - located on the Main Cliff section of Cala Marçal. Photo: Beail Collection

Cala Marçal — Main Cliff

1) Rope ladder exit
2) Gully exit

Main Cliff
The Main Cliff consists of a great selection of juggy routes in the mid-6s. The right-hand side of the cliff has a good traverse which is used to gain the start of most of the routes. Although the Main Cliff is 16m high, all but a few routes (*Scorpion* and *The Fat Crab*) ease off considerably in their upper halves. The routes do sometimes get greasy on hot days, so it is ideal to have a sea breeze to hand.

❸ The Fat Crab — 6a+ S1
Traverse onto the main wall and climb the crack-line to half height below a bulging wall. Move out right to better holds, and up to the overlap. Traverse back left until you reach a gap in the lip. Pull onto a small shelf and reach for the top. *Photo p.71.*
FA. James Cole 6.2005

❹ Hellraiser — 6b S2
Climb the rib and watch the ledge below. Snatchy moves lead to the upper line of *The Fat Crab*. From the break, move right onto a ledge and then the top.
FA. Daimon Beail 9.2007

❺ ET v Predator — 6b S1
Traverse right under *The Fat Crab* and continue along to pass a sharp protruding fin. This leaves you under an overlapping wall. Climb the left side of this wall to pass the right-hand side of the cave, and continue much more easily to the top.
FA. James Cole 6.2005

❻ Mortal Combat — 6b+ S0
A great find with good positions throughout. Attack the overlapping wall on good holds to the lip. Pull over the lip and trend left to a large jug. Climb the rib from here, with much easier ground on the upper section. *Photo p.75.*
FA. Daimon Beail 6.2005

❶ Dead Prawn — 6a S2
Follow the arete with fingery moves into the scoop near the top. Take care when leaving the second ledge.
FA. Bernard Exley 14.10.2012

❷ Scorpion — 6b S1
Nice wall-climbing. A long reach to a good pocket halfway up. *Photo p.69.*
FA. Bernard Exley 14.10.2012

Main Cliff Cala Marçal

3) Small cave exit

Approach (map and overview p.68) - The routes on the left-hand side are reached by an easy down-climb (4a) and then traversing right. On the right another easy descent (4a) will get you to all the routes, along with the traverse of *The Odyssey*. These descents are not DWS climbing so abseil if you are unsure.

Exits – Needs a close inspection prior to your ascent.
1) A rope ladder at the first way down.
2) Some tricky, sharp moves exiting around the gully area and a traverse leftwards from there.
3) A possible exit at the small cave just to the northeast.

7 Homerophobia 5c S0
Drop down to sea level and traverse left around an arete and up into a small cave. Exit steeply on the right and head up to the ledge just shy of the top.
FA. John Bull 2.5.2008

8 The Odyssey 5a S0
36m. A nice traverse along the lower break, past a cave to the arete, where an easy-angled flake leads you to the top.
FA. Daimon Beail 6.2005

The rest of the climbs are approached along The Odyssey.

9 Canada 4a S1
From the base of the easy way down, step up into the groove and follow the curving flake to its end. Easy climbing remains.
FA. Daimon Beail 6.2005

10 Aquafresh 6c S1
A tight bit of good wall climbing. Locate a two-finger pocket and climb the crimpy wall above. The top-out is much easier.
FA. Daimon Beail 6.2005

11 Lady Boys 5c S0
Excellent climbing. Find the large hold under the roof and pull onto the slotted face above. The slot holds are all huge.
FA. James Cole 6.2005

12 Higher than the Sun 6a S0
A tricky start leads to excellent climbing on good holds.
FA. James Cole 6.2005

13 Tekken 2 .... 7a S0
Climb the roof on pockets with difficulty to gain the upper wall.
FA. Bob Hickish, 9.2006

14 Groove Rider .... 6a+ S0
To the right of the small roof is a crack-line. Jamming and laybacking lead you to the top.
FA. Daimon Beail 6.2005

15 Hoy Voy de Guiri 6a S1
Climb the bulge just to the left of where *The Odyssey* drops down into the cave. Easier climbing leads right above the roof. Two alternative finishes are both the same grade as the original.
FA. Nora Dorian 7.2008

16 Hip-Hop to the Top .... 6a+ S0
Climb out of the lower cave to a groove leading to a small roof. Traverse right under this then gain the wall above.
FA. Nora Dorian 7.2008

17 Time 6a S0
Thin diagonal moves to the upper right-hand corner and a small flat ledge above your head. Easier climbing leads to the top.
FA. Daimon Beail 6.2005

Cala Marçal — Small Headland and The Cala Wall

Small Headland
To the right of the exit point of *The Odyssey*, the wall decreases in height and leads into a small bay made by a headland with a low back wall.

❶ Marçal Morceau .... ☐ **6a** *SO*
Left of this back wall is an arete. Descend easily to the left of the arete (Looking in) and traverse right onto and up the arete.
FA. John Bull 5.5.2008

❷ Oaker's Lab .... ☐ **5c** *SO*
On the small headland. Make a short descent to the left of the headland and traverse rightwards along the break-line before heading diagonally up more steeply to finish.
FA. John Bull 2.5.2008

The Cala Wall
Some good gentle traversing in the main cala with some alternative finishes.

Approach (map and overview p.68) - Make a short walk north (around the last house) from the parking. Drop down to the cliff edge to the start of *The Marçal Traverse* which is where the cliff increases in height and the rock changes from sharp grey to orange.

Exit - Sort a rope out to help you get out of the water here, or take a long swim back along the cliff to a metal ladder bolted onto the side of the cliff.

❸ The Marçal Traverse .... ☆2 ☐ **5c** *SO*
30m+. A short and easy traverse. Join the sea cliff where the sharp grey walls finish and the delights of the orange juggy wall start. Follow this past the roof section and exit at the small platform where it gets sharp again.
FA. James Cole, Sue Hazel, Daimon Beail, F.Fulcher 6.2005

❹ Art God .... ☐ **6a** *SO*
An alternative exit for *The Marçal Traverse* over the left side of the prow. It can also be reached by traversing in from the left.
FA. John Bull 2.5.2008

❺ Rat Dog .... ☆1 ☐ **6a** *SO*
An alternative exit for *The Marçal Traverse* over the prow and finishing mostly on its right. It can also be reached from the left.
FA. James Cole 6.2005

❻ Dolphins are Friendlier than Yaks ☐ **3a** *SO*
30m+. The easiest recorded traverse on the island.
FA. Richard Goodey and Sarah Allard 18.8.2023

There are numerous possibilities on the other side of the bay, below the white 'JS Cape Colom Hotel' - most are short and unappealing. One line tackles the small cave in that vicinity.

❼ Colomic Irrigation .... ☐ **6a+** *SO*
Traverse through the cave in either direction.

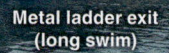

Bernard Exley hanging out on the fantastic *Mortal Combat* (6b+) - *p.72* - on the Main Cliff of Cala Marçal. Photo: Beail Collection

Cala Brafia

| Grade Spread | - | 9 | 8 | 3 | - |

A great venue; *Stigmata* is the classic of the crag but there is a great variety of worthwhile routes dotted along the Main Wall - enough for a good day trip or two. The shady Cala Wall also has a good selection of easier climbs making it an appealing venue for less experienced DWS climbers, with the added attraction that the crag is usually very quiet. Most of the routes on Main Wall start from a break and are reached by traversing in from either side.

Approach
Cala Brafia is just south of Cala Marçal and some 22km south of Porto Cristo. From the Ma-4014 coastal road, turn eastwards along the Ma-4010 to Porto Colom, turn eastwards along the Ma-4010 to Porto Colom or the next junction to the south which is also well-signed. Then follow signs south to Cala Marçal and drop down to the beach. From here, swing around the bay and drive up the hill. Continue up the hill (veering leftwards onto the one-way system) until you come to two marked pedestrian crossings close together followed by a turning on your right. Follow this (Carrer Fotja) to the end, where you find a turning circle and a dirt road. Park here on the road, keeping the turning circle and dirt road clear. There are a few additional spaces further down the dirt track but these are limited. Follow the dirt road on foot until it curves round to the right. In front of you is a narrow path, right of some gated entrances to properties, which leads down to a beach (this is a nudist beach so please respect people's privacy). Continue across the beach and head along the right-hand side of the bay to the headland where you will find the crag.

Conditions
The Main Wall is exposed and dries quickly but steep overhanging sections are prone to condensation so a breeze is always useful. It stays in the sun for most of the day. The Cala Wall is much more shady, only seeing the sun in the early morning.

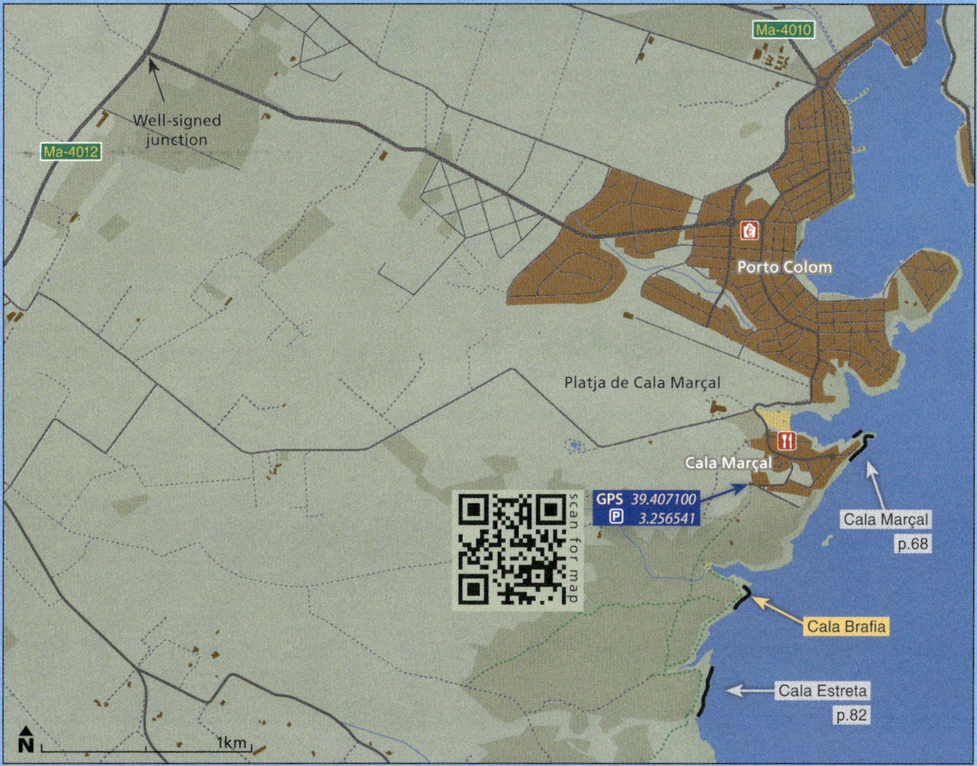

Cala Brafia 77

Cala Brafia — Main Wall

Main Wall

The Main Wall is split into to two halves. The left side is probably the most attractive section and is home to the overhanging prow of *Stigmata*, which for some is worth the trip alone. The right-hand side of the wall has a selection of routes with roof starts in one form or another which are fun but short lived. There is still a large collection of bird dung along the break which can be avoided.

Approach (map and overview p.77) - All the routes on the Main Wall are best approached by the *Photon Traverse* which is a grade 4 up to where it drops down past *Owl Cave* and into *Stigmata*. Routes that come in from the left are reached by down climbing 20m to the left of the main wall to a large ledge and heading right from there.

Exits - Rope exit points are dotted around either side of the Main Wall but must be installed before attempting any lines otherwise exiting could be difficult.

❶ Speed of Light........ 7a *S0*
A very good pocketed approach start to reversing the *Photon Traverse* which is approached by down climbing 20m left of the main wall to a large ledge. Walk right to the end of the ledge to where you can down climb to the lower wall and start the route.
FA. Pete Robins, Dan McManus 2023

❷ Toxic Musculinity .... 7a+ *S0*
Head to the big horizontal slot left of the big hold on *Stigmata* and pull hard onto the upper wall on crimps.
FA. Remus Knowles 10.10.2024

❸ Stigmata .... 6c+ *S0*
Traversing left until you are under a mean overhanging bulge. Follow a series of jugs and ledges to reach the upper face. Move up and right via some technical moves to finish. *Photo p.81*.
FA. Daimon Beail 5.10.2011

❹ Photon Reverse......... 7a+ *S0*
A left-to-right low down version of the *Photon Traverse*. Slightly eliminate and escapable.
FA. Felix Coxwell and others 29.9.2024

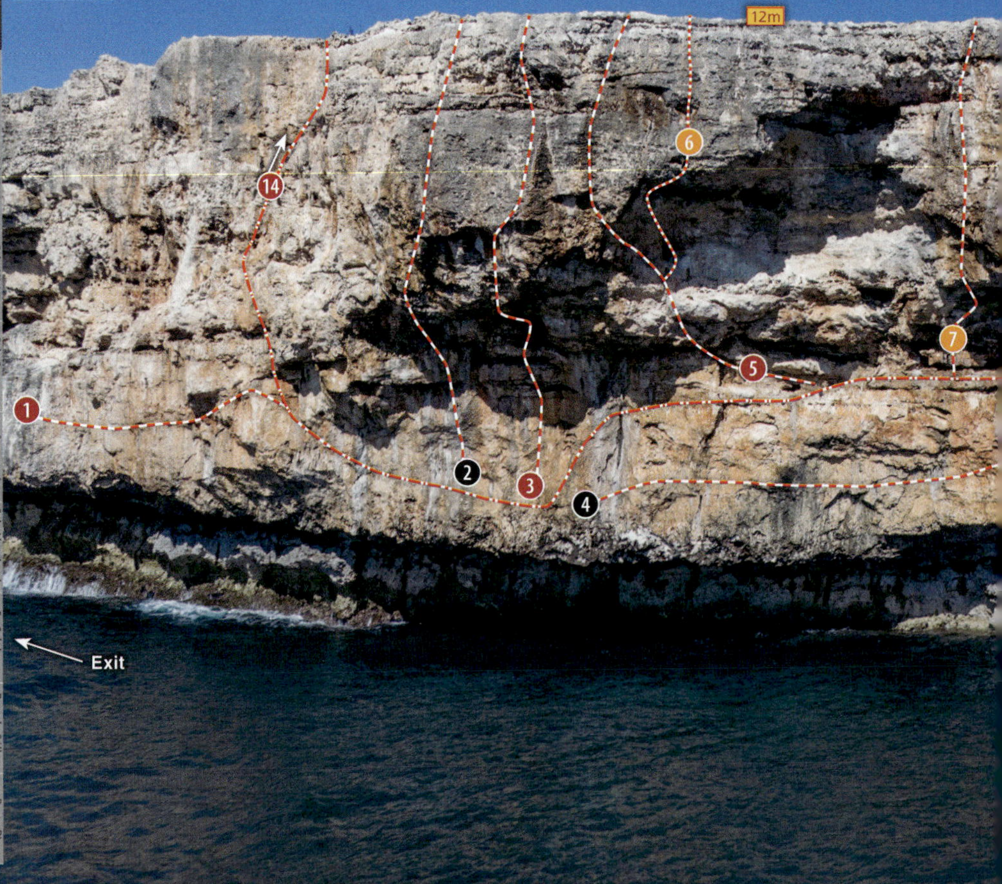

Main Wall Cala Brafia

⑤ Owl Cave 6b *S1*
An enjoyable outing around the blind corner and some fingery moves on the face. *Photo p.80.*
FA. Daimon Beail 6.10.2011

⑥ Up Quark .... 6a+ *S1*
From the ledge/cave, attack the roof via a letter-box on the lip.
FA. Bernard Exley 6.10.2011

⑦ Eye Poker .... 6a+ *S0*
The far left line over the roof via two nicely placed pockets.
FA. Daimon Beail 5.10.2011

⑧ Span-tastic 6c *S0*
Make a big span from good undercuts to a slopey jug, then haul to the top. A bit of a one-move-wonder.
FA. Adam Brown 6.10.2011

⑨ Rest Day 7b *S0*
Attack the roof, finishing with a hard rockover from some small sharp handholds.
FA. Tom Le Fanu 6.10.2011

⑩ Tevatron 6c *S0*
An easily identifiable line breaking up the steep roof climbs either side of it.
FA. Bernard Exley 6.10.2011

⑪ Neutrino .... 6b+ *S0*
Steeper and harder climbing to the right of *Tevatron* leads to a good mantel.
FA. Bernard Exley 6.10.2011

⑫ Electron .... 6a+ *S0*
The left side of the block using some wild heel-hooks.
FA. Bernard Exley 6.10.2011

⑬ Atom 5c *S0*
The right side of the block.
FA. Bernard Exley 6.10.2011

⑭ Photon Traverse 6b *S0*
A right-to-left traverse and also the easy line to all the routes on this wall. It's only a grade 4 for most of the way, with the last section just past *Stigmata* pushing the grade up to **6b**.
FA. Bernard Exley 6.10.2011

Cala Brafia — Cala Wall

Cala Wall

Tucked round to the right-hand side of the main face is a smaller wall of approximately 10m. It presents a selection of good easier routes in a shady setting. The roof climbs can be greasy if the weather is calm. Best to try this in the afternoon with a bit of a breeze.

Approach (map and overview p.77) - The main approach is from the right (looking in). The first two routes should be approached from the left by easy down-climb.

1 Neutron 5a S0
A short climb on the left side of the wall.
FA. Bernard Exley 6.10.2011

2 Third Time Lucky .... 6c+ S0
Probably the best here with reachy moves over the left side of the roof.
FA. Bernard Exley 8.10.2012

3 Given .... 6a+ S0
Climb the groove and over the roof using jugs.
FA. Michal Becker 8.10.2012

4 New Born 6a S0
The right-hand side of the roof.
FA. Daimon Beail 8.10.2012

5 Blue Bikini 5a S0
The white slab moving up and right to an easy finish.
FA. Emma Beail 8.10.2012

6 Black Jack 6a S0
The black streak.
FA. Bernard Exley 8.10.2012

Daimon Beail emerging from *Owl Cave* (6b) - *p.79* - on the Main Wall of Cala Brafia.
Photo: Beail Collection

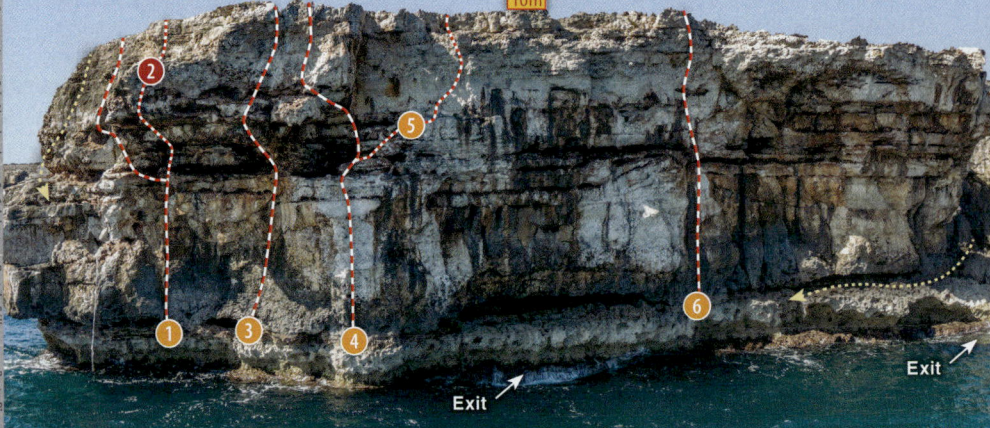

Michal Becker tackling one of the best lines at Cala Brafia, *Stigmata* (6c+) - *p.78* - on the Main Wall. Plenty of powerful climbing up to the final crimpy face where the moves cause many to take flight.
Photo: Beail Collection

Cala Estreta

Grade Spread | 1 | 2 | 4 | 2 | 2

The amazing Cala Estreta cave is a fortress of solitude for the DWS connoisseur. Early exploration in 2006 resulted in one amazing climb being established - *An Inconvenient Roof*. It took another five years before further development took place with a set of more amenable climbs which put it on the map. It is less popular than other destinations along the east coast and the cave may put many off. *As Good as it Gets* is worth seeking out as well as the other additional outings found along the wings that could make your trip worthwhile.

Approach
Cala Estreta can be approached from Cala Marçal or Cala Sa Nau.

Cala Marçal approach - From the Ma-4014 coastal road, turn eastwards along the Ma-4010 to Porto Colom, turn eastwards along the Ma-4010 to Porto Colom or the next junction to the south which is also well-signed. Then follow signs south to Cala Marçal and drop down to the beach. From here, swing around the bay and drive up the hill. Continue up the hill (veering leftwards onto the one-way system) until you come to two marked pedestrian crossings close together followed by a turning on your right. Follow this (Carrer Fotja) to a turning circle and a dirt road. Park here on the road. Follow the dirt road on foot until it curves round to the right. Take a small path straight ahead (right of some gated entrances to properties) which leads down to a beach and then onto the crag Cala Brafia. From here continue on to the next tiny bay of Cala Estreta and walk down the right side. The cliff rises to the right and the cave lies beneath its peak.

Cala Sa Nau approach - Drive south on the Ma-4012 coast road until you come to a small village called S'Horta. This point can also be reached from Santanyí driving north. Turn left, following signs to Cala Ferrera and after a short distance, fork left towards Cala Sa Nau. Fork left again (signed 'Cami de Cala sa Nau') and follow this road to its end and a large car park. From the parking, cross the beach and find a path that leads across the headland directly to Cala Estreta. The path weaves, but once you reach the cliff, head left (looking out).

Conditions
The crag faces east and catches the sun from morning to mid-afternoon. Some of the lines on either side of the cave stay dry for the majority of the time, but the inner cave and roof need a few days of light breeze to dry out. The left side of the cave has a platform which might hinder the starts to possible future lines, so take care. Also the traverse in from the right side has a precarious drop-down move near a sharp knife-edge hold that could cause damage if you come into contact with it.

Daimon Beail climbing *As Good as it Gets* (6b) - *p.84* - on the left side of the Cave at Cala Estreta. This is a great line with a slightly challenging upper section. Photo: Beail Collection

Cala Estreta — Cave

① **The Great Escape** 4c *S1*
20m to the right (looking out) of the cave is a narrow section of cliff. Approach by down climbing the left-hand side (looking out) of the face with care. Keep an eye on the lower ramp.
FA. Bernard Exley 5.10.2011

② **As Good as it Gets** .... 6b+ *S0*
Lovely jug-pulling to the top with a mildly technical bit in the middle. *Photo p.83*.
FA. Bernard Exley 5.10.2011

Cave — Cala Estreta

Cave

The Cave at Cala Estreta has now seen the much needed development it so deserves, though further potential remains. The main cave is prone to condensation so make sure you visit on a day when there is a light breeze to bring it into condition. The routes to the edges of the cave are generally drier.

Approach (map p.82) - For *An Inconvenient Roof*, traverse in from either side or dry-bag swim in. The routes to the right are reached by traversing in from the right. Descend (ideally using a rope) a slight groove to a shallow recess where you can stash chalk and gear.

Exits - Set up a water exit below the recess for gear and chalk to the right of the cave. There are also many exit possibilities in the centre and to the left of the main cave.

③ **An Inconvenient Roof** ... 8b S2
Forearms beware! From the right side of the ledge, climb up about 5m on jugs to a big scary move to a large pocket (watching the starting ledge below you - hence the S grade). Move right through the roof on a series of big holds until you reach the crux on the headwall involving a tricky two-finger undercut for the right hand. If successful, continue up and rightwards to the top.
FA. Ethan Pringle 9.2006

④ **The Bull and the Bride** .... 6b+ S0
The rising traverse approached from a little way along *Hung Drawn and Quartered*. It can be a bit dirty.
FA. Tom Le Fanu 5.10.2011

⑤ **Mia Julia** 8a S2
A powerful roof climb gained from *The Bull and the Bride*.
FA. Michael Piccolruaz 2023

⑥ **Caro Line** 7c S2
A slightly easier roof climb compared to its neighbour.
FA. Jernej Kruder 2023

⑦ **Long Traverse** .... 7a+ S2
Wind your way around the roof and traverse the lip of the cave
FA. Jernej Kruder 2023

⑧ **The Land that Time Forgot** ... 6c S0
Steep but juggy roof climbing across the lip. Exit where things get out of hand and you are forced to go up through a series of slopers.
FA. Daimon Beail 5.10.2011

⑨ **Force of Nature** 6b S0
Climb *The Land that Time Forgot* under the roof until a handle. Head up over the roof from that point and onto some lovely (but spicy) rails.
FA. Daimon Beail 5.10.2011

⑩ **Planet POB** 6a S0
An easy jug-fuelled line that is short lived but well worth doing.
FA. Daimon Beail 5.10.2011

⑪ **Hung Drawn and Quartered** .. 6a S1
A right-to-left traverse of the cave with a steep start that soon gives way to easier climbing the further in you go. Just remember to breathe in when passing the spike! The route is usually started just below the recess. Head left towards a hole which can be easily crawled through. Take care when passing the spike in the centre of the cave that gives the route its name.
FA. Bernard Exley 5.10.2011

86 | **Cala Sa Nau**

| Grade Spread | 3 | 7 | 10 | 5 | 4 |

Cala Sa Nau is one of the big three hard DWS venues on the island. It was made famous in 2003 when Chris Sharma and Klem Loskot added two major lines in the Hupolup Kempf Cave that captured the climbing world's imagination, though the grades and extreme nature made this the preserve of the elite-level climber. Since then, development of the Cave has stalled with only one newer route being added in the next twenty years. The wider appeal of the area was increased the next year when a team of climbers from the UK developed the Virgin Area with a good spread of more accessible graded routes. The traverses on the far side of the bay add to the appeal, especially since they are well sheltered when the sea is rough. There is also a lovely beach and bar near the parking which is a great place to relax after a day's climbing.

Approach

Drive south on the Ma-4012 coast road until you come to a small village called S'Horta. This point can also be reached from Santanyí driving north. Turn left, following signs to Cala Ferrera and after a short distance, fork left towards Cala Sa Nau. Fork left again (signed 'Cami de Cala sa Nau') and follow this road to its end and a large car park. On your return you are sent on a one-way system on these approach roads back to S'Horta. From the parking, walk along the right-hand side of the bay until you reach some steps cut into the rock. From here, cut across right to reach the Virgin Area and then head left to reach the Hupolup Kempf Cave and Bounty Sector. For the bay traverses, head up the left-hand side of the bay until you can see an orange-looking wall.

Cala Sa Nau 87

Conditions
The Hupolup Kempf Cave stays relatively dry due to its steepness but it will still retain its greasiness if there is no breeze, however its exposed position means that dampness can disappear quickly in such conditions. The Virgin Area is more sheltered which is beneficial when seas are a bit choppy but the small cave does hold dampness. The Bay Traverses are all well sheltered from any rough seas.

Cala Sa Nau — Virgin Area

Virgin Area

A good area with some steep stuff in the cave that can get damp, and some gentler offerings on the wall to the right.
Approach (map and overview p.87) - *Virgins are Only Human* is gained by a simple down-climb and a little walk along a ledge until you start climbing. *Attack of the Spindly Killer Fish* to *Little Fish* are traditionally approached by reversing *Frogger* or *C++*. *Captain Black* and *What a Small World* are reached by making your way carefully down the left side of the cave (looking in) to sea level where you can traverse into the cave to where the routes start.
Exit - Under the start of *Virgins are Only Human* for all routes.

❶ Virgins are Only Human........ 6a+ S0
Walk up the simple ramp until you reach the roof near the end. Traverse out right and nip up the right side of the roof.
FA. Bernard Exley 10.2004

❷ Killer Virgin......... 6b S0
At the point *Virgins Are only Human* gets steep, traverse down and right past a hole inside the cave and into (but avoiding the steep crux section of) *Attack of the Spindly Killer Fish*. Reverse this to its start.
FA. Crispin Waddy 1.9.2013

❸ Losing My Virginity.. 6b+ S0
Potential for an early wetting unless your forearms are in good shape. Traverse the lip of the cave and exit back onto the ramp. Exit easily left back down the ramp.

❹ What a Small World..... 7b S0
An alternative start to the line of *Captain Black* that tackles the roof directly from the pillar feature at the end of the ledge.
FA. Sam Harvie 17.10.2013

❺ Captain Black... 7a S0
From within the cave, lean across and reach the bulge on the roof and some good holds. Pull onto the roof and climb right on pockets, crimps and jugs to eventually gain the lip where the final stretch can kick shorties off. Exit easily left back down the ramp of *Virgins are Only Human*.

Virgin Area **Cala Sa Nau** 89

Down climb Frogger to reach the starts of the following climbs.

6 Cave Route 7a S0
When conditions are right it's possible to traverse into the cave and climb a big flake through the centre and finish on the ledge of *Virgins are Only Human*.
FA. Henry Crawley 26.6.2022

7 Attack of the Spindly Killer Fish
.... 7a+ S0
Climb the arete on the right-hand side of the cave to a break below the bulge. Move up and right to make some hard moves over the bulge. *Photo p.93.*
FA. Nic Ward 6.2006

8 Gen Lock 6b S0
Climb your way up to the roof and locate some hidden buckets, then power to the top. Can be started from water level.
FA. Daimon Beail 10.2004

9 I Tell Thee 4c S0
Start as for *Gen Lock* then make a rising traverse right to exit.
FA. Daimon Beail 10.2004

10 Coldron................... 5a S0
A direct variation of *I Tell Thee*.
FA. James Cole 10.2004

11 Frogger 4c S1
From just right the start of *Coldron*, traverse rightwards to the arete and continue right again to climb the flake to the top. Watch out for the little ledge below.
FA. Heidi Spets 10.2004

12 C++ 4c S0
Start as for *Frogger*, then climb the faint arete.
FA. Peter Brown 10.2004

13 Little Fish.................. 5c S1
Start as for *Frogger* and make your way along the cliff until you reach the sandy arete, which you finish up - keep away from the ledge out right. Halfway through the traverse is a little cave. The climbing here is above a small ledge, so take care!
FA. Heidi Spets 10.2004

Cala Sa Nau — Hupolup Kempf Cave

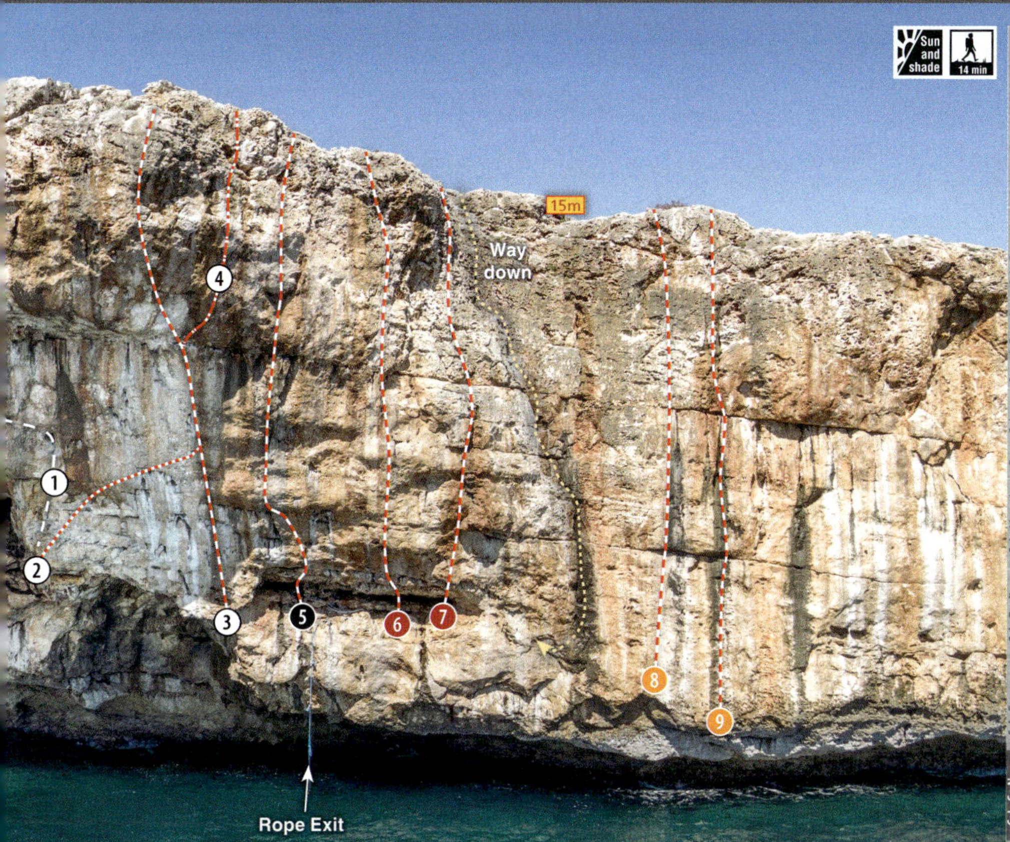
Sun and shade
14 min
15m
Way down
Rope Exit

Hupolup Kempf Cave

Hard and intimidating routes for the more daring deep water soloist. Luckily, things ease off on the right-hand side.
Approach (map and overview p.87) - Either scramble down the back side (grade 4) and traverse off left (facing the rock) and into the back side of the cave - photo left - or down climb (grade 5) between *Notatrocity* and *Scalfament*.
Exit - Exits are tricky in rough water and the crag should be avoided in these conditions. In calmer seas, it is easy to clamber out directly under the mouth of the large cave.

① Hupolup Kempf...... 8b S2
The shape of things to come. Klem Loskot's testpiece tackles the right-hand side of the cave to the roof which is crossed using crimpy holds.
FA. Klem Loskot 2003

② The Weather Man - Left-hand .... 8a+ S2
A left-hand start to the next route.
FA. Chris Sharma 2003

③ The Weather Man.... 8a+ S2
Similar ground to *Hupolup Kempf* but mildly easier. Nevertheless it requires an immense amount of mind control when making those final moves to the jug.
FA. Chris Sharma 2003

④ Salty Beverage.. 8b S2
A hard direct finish to *The Weather Man*.
FA. Jernej Kruder 2018

⑤ Vadage............ 7b S1
Make a direct ascent to the bulge and continue over it, making some harder moves to reach easier ground.

⑥ Cheers Chartle.......... 6c+ S0
The bulging wall on chalked-up pockets is a popular one.

⑦ Notatrocity .... 6b+ S0
The first line to the left (looking in) of the way down.

⑧ Scalfament 6a S1
Follow the left-hand dark streak to the top.

⑨ Scalfament 2.................. 6a+ S1
Follow the right-hand dark streak to the top.

Porto Cristo
P. Cristo Novo
Cala Barques
Cova d. Burador
Porto Colom
Cala Marçal
Cala Brafia
Cala Estreta
Cala Sa Nau
Cala Mitjana
Cala Serena
Santanyí
Cala Llombards
Sa Calobra
Port de Sóller
Porto Pi

Cala Sa Nau — Bounty Sector

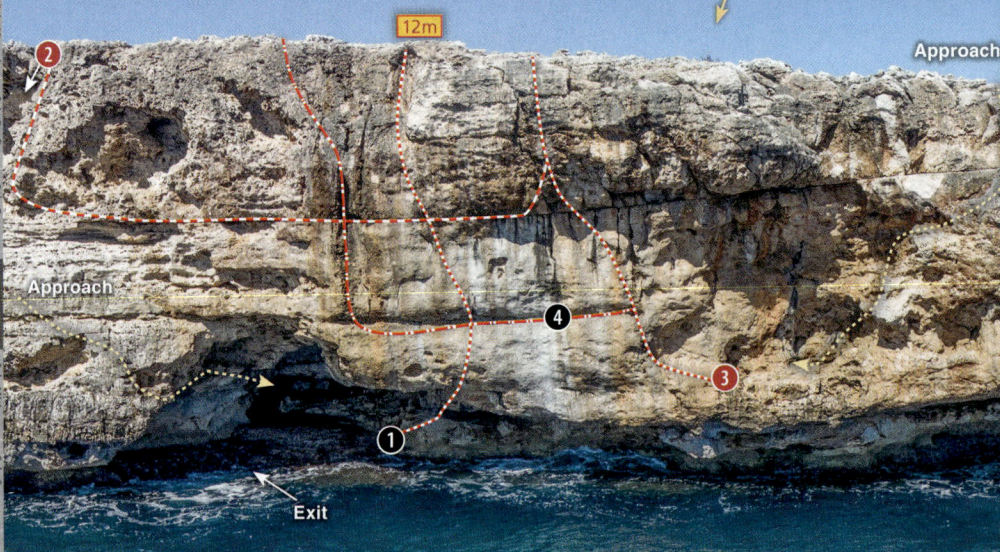

Bounty Sector
The face continuing right (looking in) from the Hupolup Kempf Cave decreases in height to lead to a nice wall with some good lines which are often overlooked.

Approach (map p.87) - Approximately 150m right (looking in) of the Hupollup Kempf Cave close to the tip of the headland. Down climb easily to the right of the area.

Exit - Install a rope exit or make a tricky climb out of the cave below the face.

❶ **Lost Property Attrocity** .... 7a+ S0
Traverse in to the sea-level cave. Climb out on big pockets and cross *Westatrocity* then up the headwall.
FA. Pete Robins 2018

❷ **Bounty** 6c S0
A good left-to-right traverse. Climb down into the scoop and traverse the finger-rail to join the last part of *Under a Dark Sky*.
FA. Bernard Exley 2005

❸ **Under a Dark Sky** 6b S0
Climb up and left to a series of flutings and a break under the roof. Move slightly left and over the lip on good holds.
FA. Daimon Beail 2004

❹ **Westatrocity** .... 7a+ S0
Start up *Under a Dark Sky* and traverse the lower break beneath *Bounty* right to left, along the barrel-shaped wall. Just before the lip of the cave, head up the orange streak and direct to the top.
FA. Sam Whittaker 12.9.2002

Cala Sa Nau

Tom Le Fanu on *Attack of the Spindly Killer Fish* (7a+) - *p.89* - at Virgin Area of Cala Sa Nau.
Photo: Beail Collection

Cala Sa Nau — Bay Traverses

Bay Traverses

For those who have climbed on the Virgin Area and exhausted the routes available at the friendlier grades, there are three long traverses on the far side of the bay that should be appealing. The first two can be found on the small headland approximately 100m from the beach.

Approach (map and overview p.87) - All three routes are easily reached via numerous paths that run from the beach and along the north side of the bay.

Exits - The exits are often close to the start of traverses. Have ropes and equipment in place before venturing out.

❶ Orange Wall.......... 6a+ SO
20m. On the east face of the same headland sheltering the beach from the open water is an orange wall of good rock that can be traversed along the central break-line and finished just right of the small cave.

❷ Beachside Traverse...... 6a SO
50m. Traverse the south-facing orange wall on the left-hand side of the bay (about 100m out) which can easily be seen by looking directly east from the beach. Begin by traversing through a small cave to an easier wall until the wall bulges. Beyond this a large ledge can be found. Top out easily from here.

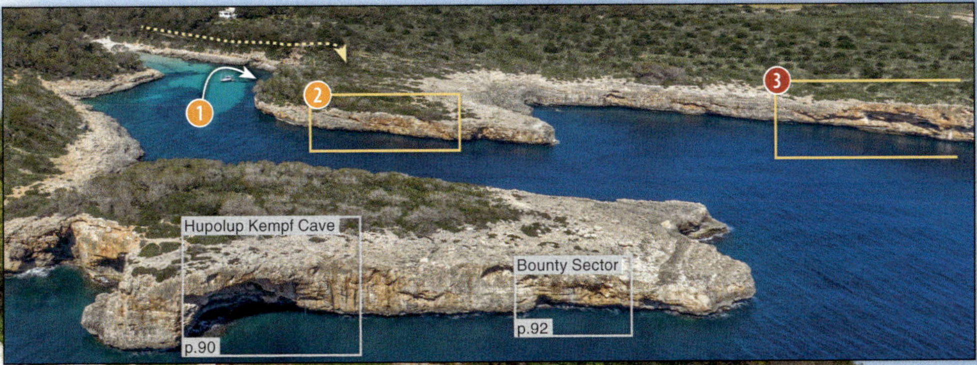

Bay Traverses — Cala Sa Nau

③ The Dino Egg Traverse ... 6b+ *SO*
200m. A final harder traverse can be found further east, past the small headland on a rising orange wall on the left side of the bay. It is a long and relatively easy left-to-right traverse with one or two difficult bits which can be bypassed easily. The height of the wall increases but the finish is easy on a variety of escape lines. A hidden fossilised 'dino egg' can be found along the way. An average grade of **6b+** has been given, but you can make it as easy as **6a**, or as hard as **7a+** if you take the lowest line.
FA. Daimon Beail, James Cole, Pete Brown, Bernard Exley, Heidi Spets 10.2004

Cala Mitjana

Grade Spread | - | 9 | 12 | 7 | 7

Cala Mitjana was amongst the original big four venues on the island. International climbing teams visited as early as 2002, but without any significant additions or recorded lines apart from the establishment of the then project *Animal Magnetism*. Since then its popularity has increased significantly with the addition of the smaller, fun and bouldery Rich Bitch Cave which is popular today. The true star of the four walls is the Wall of Illuminations which hosts mostly hard climbs and some excellent more attainable grades. The cliff rises the further right you go (looking in) to eventually arrive at the Kraken Wall, an extremely intimidating venue with three climbs geared towards the more advanced deep water soloer. Right again is Terry Wall which is exposed and has a wild feeling when climbing there. Although the grades are not that hard, the walls are high, and completion of any of these lines is very satisfying indeed!

Approach

Cala Mitjana has the same parking as Cala Sa Nau. Drive south on the Ma-4012 coast road until you come to a small village called S'Horta. This point can also be reached from Santanyí driving north. Turn left, following signs to Cala Ferrera and, after a short distance, fork left towards Cala Sa Nau. Fork left again (signed 'Cami de Cala sa Nau') and follow this road to its end and a large car park. On your return you are sent on a one-way system on these approach roads back to S'Horta. From the parking, make your way over to the Virgin Area at Cala Sa Nau (p.86) and follow the rocky path uphill along the coast towards a wall. At the wall, ignore the sign to Cala Mitjana heading back inland, but instead proceed to follow the vague path along the flats and then back down (cutting through a well trodden vegetated area for speed) to the Cala Mitjana climbing areas - the ship's mast (which is what helps identify this area) sits just to the side of the Wall of Illuminations. Most of the routes are reached by easy down-climbs.

Cala Mitjana

GPS 39.392369, 3.246637

Conditions

Rich Bitch Cave and Kraken Wall are good options for dealing with northeasterly swells, whereas Terry Wall and Wall of Illuminations are a bit more open to the elements. All climbs tend to stay dry apart from those which are overhanging and closer to the water - these can be greasy on hot days. Keep an eye for incoming swells and have your exit and safety plans in place.

Cala Mitjana — Rich Bitch Cave

Rich Bitch Cave

Hidden away in the bay west of the main area is a popular little cave. It isn't very high and it is sheltered from the open water making it a good option if the sea is rough. The climbing style is quite bouldery and as such lends itself to link-ups and traverses - most of these are not described here.

Approach (map and overview p.97) - Make an easy down-climb left of the cave to reach climbs 1 and 2, or down climb right of the cave and traverse left to reach climbs 3 to 10.
Exits - There is more than one exit point here so set up wherever is most convenient.

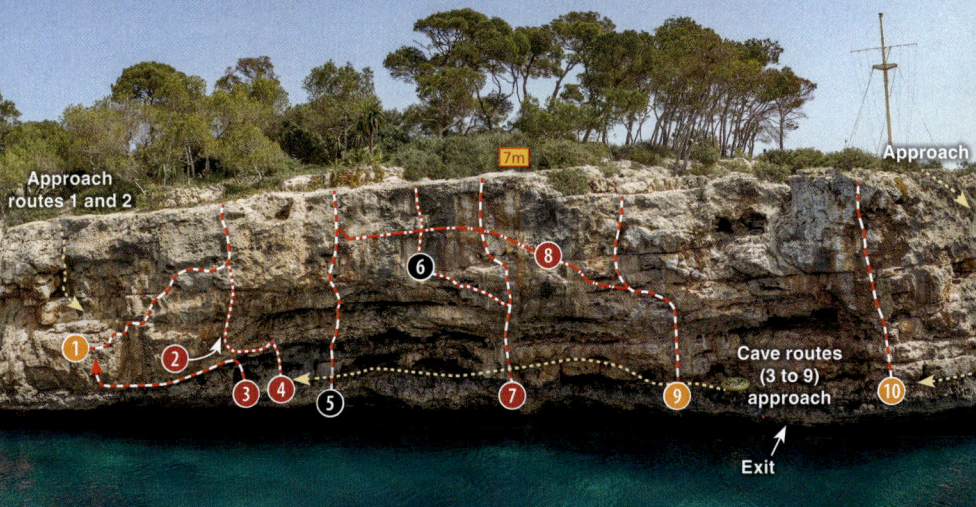

❶ The Great Sarah Psych! 5b S1
Down climb to the platform and drop down a little further. Traverse right along a rail to a good foothold. Reach around to good holds and continue up and right on good pockets. Finish direct up the wall.
FA. Daimon Beall 9.10.2016

❷ The Left Arete .... 6b+ S0
Traverse in low from the left (reversing the Low Traverse) to reach the arete. Finish up this as for Nip Slip.
FA. Jamie Sparkes 29.9.2017

❸ Low Traverse 6c S0
A super low traverse left out of the cave and onto easier ground beyond. Finish any way you like.
FA. Jamie Sparkes 29.9.2017

❹ Nip Slip 7a S0
From a small ledge, climb the roof on undercuts to the lip and head leftwards towards the side of the cave. Make some long moves on the side wall to a small edge and continue to the top on pockets and into the final moves of The Great Sarah Psych!.
FA. Robert Drynda 28.9.2017

❺ Balsa Boys .... 7a+ S0
Tackle the steepest part of the cave on a series of perfectly distanced large pockets. Reach the lip on smaller, but positive holds and heave onto the upper wall to a precarious finish.
FA. Matt Heason 9.2009

❻ Filthy Rich .... 7a+ S0
After the initial dyno on Rich Bitch, head left and up via a scooped section on the headwall.
FA. Ed Bright 31.8.2016

❼ Rich Bitch .... 6c+ S0
Start just to the right of the hole at the back of the cave on the ledge. Leap to the first pocket, and heave yourself up the wall. Make a tricky move onto a small ledge and finish with a few thin moves at the top. Photo p.3 and p.21.
FA. Ged Desforges 6.2006

❽ Johnnie Walker 6c S0
From midway up Geek, head left and traverse the lip of the cave just below the top and finish up Balsa Boys.
FA. Jonny Ashton 9.2009

❾ Geek 6a S0
A nice line up the right-hand side of the steep rock.
FA. Andy Benson 9.2009

❿ Bandy 5a S1
A nice climb up the blunt arete around 12m right of Rich Bitch. *Photo opposite.*
FA. Dan Webber 9.2009

Emma Beail enjoying an fun evening session on *Bandy* (5a) - *opposite* - at the Rich Bitch Cave at Cala Mitjana. Photo: Beail Collection

Cala Mitjana — Wall of Illuminations

Wall of Illuminations

This wall has been a secret keeper of hard lines, some remaining projects for decades though now spawned into testpieces including the famous *Animal Magnetism*.

Approach (map and overview p.97) - Descend the left side of the cave easily for the left-hand cave climbs. Those starting from the inner cave require a traverse in. *Animal Magnetism* requires an abseil in and seated set-up to start.

For climbs starting from the right, locate an easy grade 4 down-climb 10m to the right (looking in) of *Illuminations*. Traverse back with care.

❶ Midnight Mast .... 6b+ *S0*
Trickier than it looks. Needs some laybacking near the top.

❷ Mitjana Party - Left .. 6c+ *S1*
A great adventure through the main cave with a good rest in the upper small cave near the top to help regather before the finish.

❸ Mitjana Party .... 7a+ *S1*
Although the original version of the two, it is an eliminate, which unfortunately requires you to keep right of is upper cave and avoid the much needed rest. Tricky moves on the final section can kick most off at the end.

❹ Escape of Thanatos... 7c+ *S0*
Climb *Mitjana Party*, avoiding the rest in the upper cave. Traverse right along the juggy brake and finish up the final dynamic section of *Sisifo*.
FA. Ben Webber 2021

❺ Sisifo............. 8a *S0*
Exit the cave and climb through a complex series of overhangs, winding your way to the break at the lip of the cave. Move right and up to a dynamic finish.
FA. Pol Roca 2019

❻ Easyfo............... 7c *S0*
An easier finish to *Sisifo* - traverse left to avoid the final dyno.

❼ Bipolar Ape 8b *S0*
Link *Animalistic* back into *Sisifo*.
FA. Ethan Pringle 2019

Wall of Illuminations — Cala Mitjana

⑧ Animalistic — 8c SO
An incredible demonstration of dynamic ability and vision. Make your way out of the cave and fly up the wall into the remainder of *Animal Magnetism*.
FA. Pol Roca 2020

⑨ Mezmerizer — 8a+ SO
Climb *Animal Magnetism* into the final section of *Sisifo*.
FA. Martin Classen 2020

⑩ Trail Hawk — 8c SO
Climb *Animalistic* into the remainder of *Empainada*.
FA. Jonas Winter 2024

⑪ Empainada — 8b+ SO
Climb the start of *Animal Magnetism* and exit early to climb direct up the sharp thin face.
FA. Marco Muller 2023

⑫ Animal Magnetism — 8b+ SO
16 years in the making and made famous by its twin dynos. Hard climbing throughout and thus reserved only for the elite!
Photo p.23.
FA. Jernej Kruder 12.10.2018

⑬ Maximuscle — 7b SO
Traverse out leftwards from *Illuminations* onto a series of small holds and three often-damp ones. Move out left then make a reachy move up from poor footholds to tackle the wall above.

⑭ Should I Stay or Should I Go — 7c+ SO
Link *Maximuscle* into a more direct version of *New Forms*.
FA. Pol Roca 2020

⑮ New Forms — 6b+ SO
Climb *Illuminations* to the break and traverse left for about 4m to a pocketed line rising to the top. A great line.
FA. James Cole 15.6.2005

⑯ Illuminations — 6b+ SO
Probably the best line at Mitjana. Traverse left into a giant sidepull which takes you straight into the crux. Gain the break via some shallow pockets and continue up. Move left slightly into a recess and a rest, before continuing to the top.
Photo p.1 and p.105.
FA. Daimon Beail 15.6.2005

Cala Mitjana — Kraken Wall

Kraken Wall

This towering wall is a short way along from the Wall of Illuminations. It has a few reasonably graded lines at present and some impressive potential. The wall is quite high and intimidating.

Approach (map and overview p.97) - Kraken Wall is easily identified on the right of the bay and a simple down-climb and traverse rightwards take you easily under the routes.

Conditions - Kraken Wall is sheltered from the open sea which is handy if a sudden storm hits. It's also south facing so is in the sun for most of the day. Take care when starting *Enter the Kraken* and the lines leading off this, since you need to keep to the left of the jutting-out ledge until you're in the safety zone.

❶ Warm 5a *S2*
Follow the roof tiers leftwards until you reach an exit.
FA. Bernard Exley 7.10.2011

❷ Enter the Kraken .... 6b+ *S1*
Pull off the deck and up to the cave using smooth but decent holds - spotter useful for the first few moves to keep to the left of the jutting-out ledge until you are in the safety zone. From the cave, head out left up the rising ramp under the headwall in increasingly spectacular positions. Keep an eye out for the cheeky shake-out when you need it most. *Photo p.8.*
FA. Tom Le Fanu 7.10.2011

❸ Check Out 6c *S1*
Start as for *Enter the Kraken*. Climb the steep tufa to the scoop before the headwall. Climb left then make a committing move right and follow the brown streak to the top. *Photo opposite.*
FA. Bernard Exley 7.10.2011

❹ Rib Tickler .... 6c+ *S2*
Start as for *Enter the Kraken*. From the cave, head up and right past a slightly blind move. Pocket-pull your way to glory.
FA. Tom Le Fanu 7.10.2011

Bernard Exley on *Check Out* (6c) - *opposite* - on the Kraken Wall at Cala Mitjana. Photo: Beail Collection

Cala Mitjana — Terry Wall

Terry Wall
A nice collection of routes which are slightly on the high side. Fortunately they all have easier upper halves. Terry Wall has been named in memory of Terry Harrington. This wall is east facing and exposed making it quick drying and catching the morning sun.
Approach (map and overview p.97) - From beneath Kraken Wall, head right past a drop-down move on the corner and continue round onto the exposed face.

1 Terry-fied 5a *S1*
Traverse round to the dark side of the moon and climb the wall right of the arete. Then make an airy space walk up a perfectly pocketed wall.
FA. Daimon Beail 4.10.2011

2 Follow the Light 5a *S0*
The first of the lines on the slightly steeper face. Easier climbing moving up and right of the break.
FA. Michal Becker 7.10.2011

3 The Road Warrior 5c *S0*
Move slightly right of *Follow the Light* and climb the black streak to the break and hole above. Easy climbing follows.
FA. Daimon Beail 7.10.2011

4 Terry-nova .... 6a+ *S0*
A route with a loop in it to make the most out of the climbing. Traverse along the break to reach the right-hand side. Drop down and weave your way left a few metres. Now climb up, cutting through your own traverse line, to the leftward-curving flake. Tricky moves lead to an easy section.
FA. Daimon Beail 7.10.2011

5 Carpenter .... 6a+ *S0*
Continuing at the same level from the base of *Terry-nova* is a tricky traverse. Good for those not keen on the height.
FA. Adam Brown 7.10.2011

Jess Carr on *Illuminations* (6b+) - *p.101* - on the Wall of Illuminations at Cala Mitjana. Photo: Mike Hutton

Cala Serena

Cala Serena, which was origianaly developed by Miquel Riera and friends in 2003, is the most extensive DWS venue on the island, with well over a hundred routes mainly consisting of juggy low sections and thinner, technical upper walls. Despite this, it sees little attention compared to other venues but those wanting to explore an extensive area with loads of mid-grade routes will be rewarded. If you are climbing at 6b there is a bizarre number of routes, which indicates that the climbing style on many of them is quite similar. For those operating below this level, head to Sector Sosec. The cliff rises to about 18m in places but most routes finish well below this and topping out is generally okay with many routes finishing on some sort of ledge.

Access
Things have changed since Cala Serena was first developed more than 20 years ago. At that time the buildings were abandoned and access was easy. Since then, the area has seen a dramatic regeneration and is now the Beverly Hills of the east coast. This has introduced some access issues but only for a small section of cliff.

Conditions
Most of the routes are quick drying except in the cave sections where dampness can linger for a long time. Towards the late afternoon, hundreds of jellyfish have been seen streaming by. This is not a constant feature but something to watch out for.

Water Exits
Before venturing onto any of the routes, make sure you have a rope in place to get out of the water - escaping is a big problem here. Also, having an inflatable around is a good idea. Suggested water exit points are marked on the topos, but more are certainly available.

Daimon Beail enjoying one of the many excellent lines on the Sosec Area of Cala Serena - *Mano negra* (6b) - *p.119*. Photo: Beail Collection

Cala Serena

Approach

From the village of S'Horta on the Ma-4012, follow signs for Cala Ferrera and continue on the main road (past the turning for Cala Sa Nau) to a roundabout. Take the second exit still signed to Cala Ferrera and continue straight for nearly 1km.

For Sector Brazil - turn right (signed 'Cala Serena') to the southern tip and park just by the triangular junction. Centrally aligned to the triangular junction is a narrow path between houses which leads to the cliff edge.

For Sectors Bombas, Adosat and the Sa Fundacio Cave - follow the road to its end and park at the entrance to a gated community. Follow the path that leads down the right-hand side of the gated community which brings you to the cliff top above Sector Adosat.

For all other sectors - follow the road nearly to its end but turn left (signed 'Serena Sol') down a narrow road and park at its end. Walk diagonally left towards the wall and fence with a hole and cross with care. Walk towards the cliff through a maze of trees and bushes, keeping the wall and houses parallel on your right. This brings you out at the clifftop between Sector Sosec and Sector Tort and is known as the 'Fisherman's Approach'.

Note - There is no access from above Sector Adosat to Sector Sosec.

Cala Serena

Cala Serena — Sector Brazil

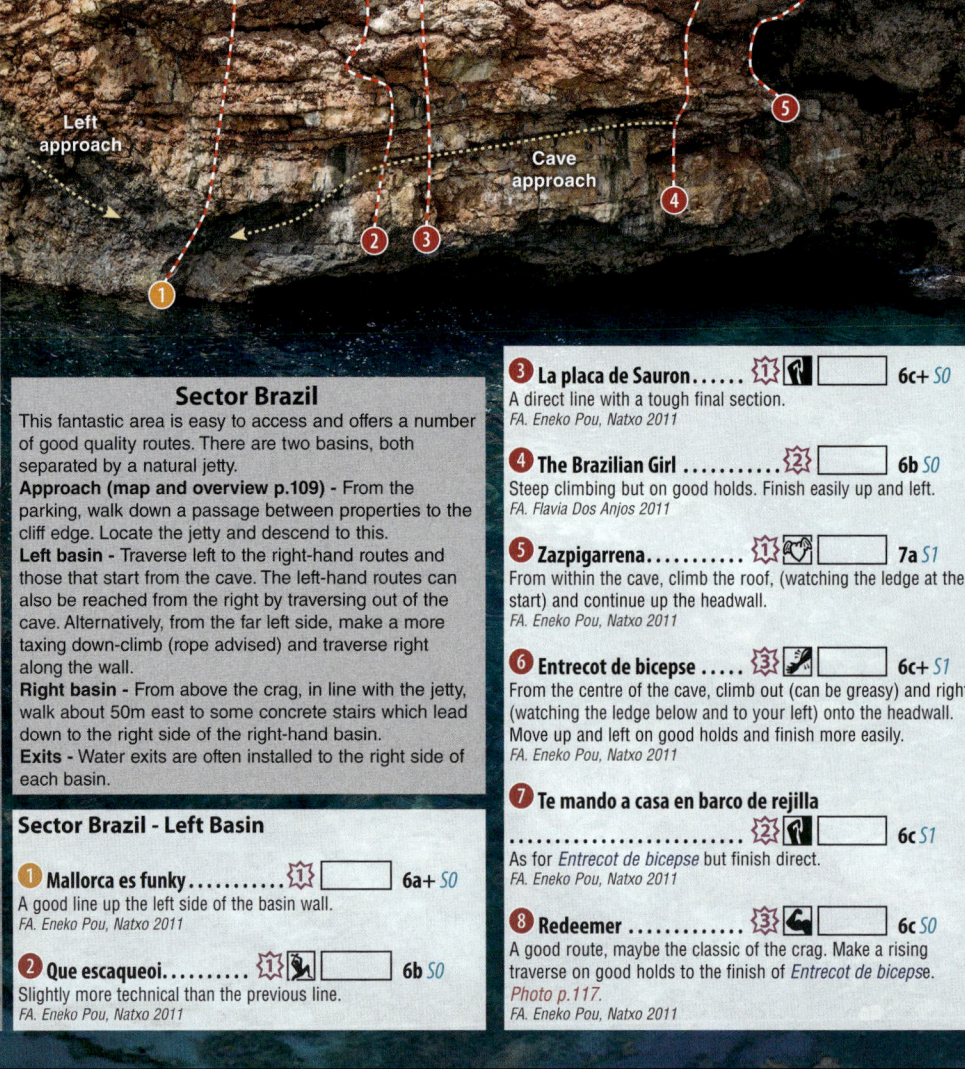

Sector Brazil

This fantastic area is easy to access and offers a number of good quality routes. There are two basins, both separated by a natural jetty.

Approach (map and overview p.109) - From the parking, walk down a passage between properties to the cliff edge. Locate the jetty and descend to this.

Left basin - Traverse left to the right-hand routes and those that start from the cave. The left-hand routes can also be reached from the right by traversing out of the cave. Alternatively, from the far left side, make a more taxing down-climb (rope advised) and traverse right along the wall.

Right basin - From above the crag, in line with the jetty, walk about 50m east to some concrete stairs which lead down to the right side of the right-hand basin.

Exits - Water exits are often installed to the right side of each basin.

Sector Brazil - Left Basin

1 Mallorca es funky .... 6a+ *S0*
A good line up the left side of the basin wall.
FA. Eneko Pou, Natxo 2011

2 Que escaqueoi. 6b *S0*
Slightly more technical than the previous line.
FA. Eneko Pou, Natxo 2011

3 La placa de Sauron ...... 6c+ *S0*
A direct line with a tough final section.
FA. Eneko Pou, Natxo 2011

4 The Brazilian Girl 6b *S0*
Steep climbing but on good holds. Finish easily up and left.
FA. Flavia Dos Anjos 2011

5 Zazpigarrena........... 7a *S1*
From within the cave, climb the roof, (watching the ledge at the start) and continue up the headwall.
FA. Eneko Pou, Natxo 2011

6 Entrecot de bicepse ..... 6c+ *S1*
From the centre of the cave, climb out (can be greasy) and right (watching the ledge below and to your left) onto the headwall. Move up and left on good holds and finish more easily.
FA. Eneko Pou, Natxo 2011

7 Te mando a casa en barco de rejilla
.... 6c *S1*
As for *Entrecot de bicepse* but finish direct.
FA. Eneko Pou, Natxo 2011

8 Redeemer 6c *S0*
A good route, maybe the classic of the crag. Make a rising traverse on good holds to the finish of *Entrecot de bicepse*.
Photo p.117.
FA. Eneko Pou, Natxo 2011

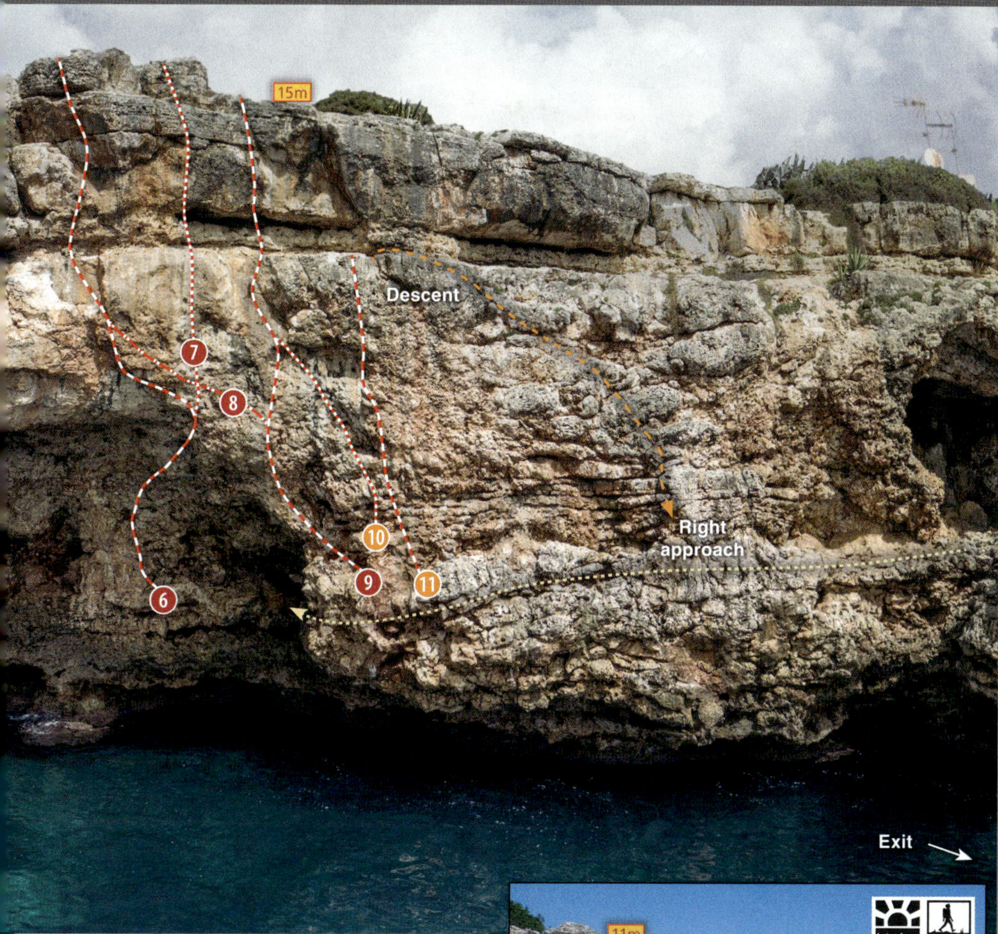

Sector Brazil — Cala Serena

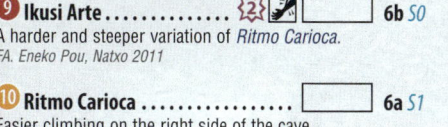

⑨ Ikusi Arte 6b S0
A harder and steeper variation of *Ritmo Carioca*.
FA. Eneko Pou, Natxo 2011

⑩ Ritmo Carioca 6a S1
Easier climbing on the right side of the cave.
FA. Eneko Pou, Natxo 2011

⑪ The Brazilian Boy 5c S2
A warm-up climb which requires some care. Descend carefully to the right.
FA. Felipe Dallorto 2011

Sector Brazil - Right Basin

⑫ A Ritmo De Samba .... 6b+ S0
A novelty climb up the centre of the right basin, moving left under the roof and finishing up a flake.
FA. Team Brazil 2012

⑬ Hier Kommt Alex 6b S1
A direct line through the roof on big holds.
FA. Lennart Seidler 7.4.2016

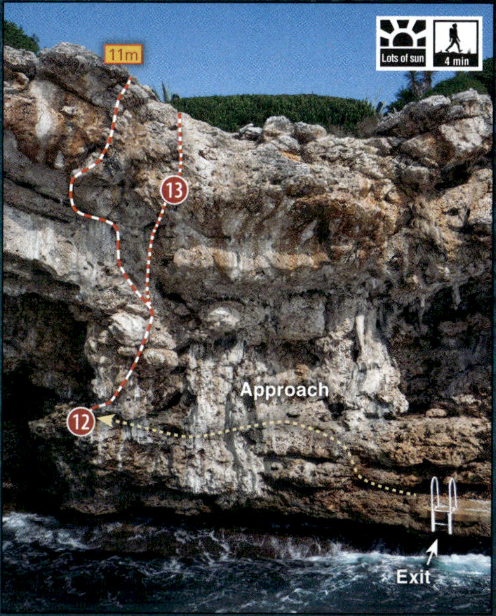

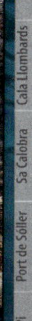

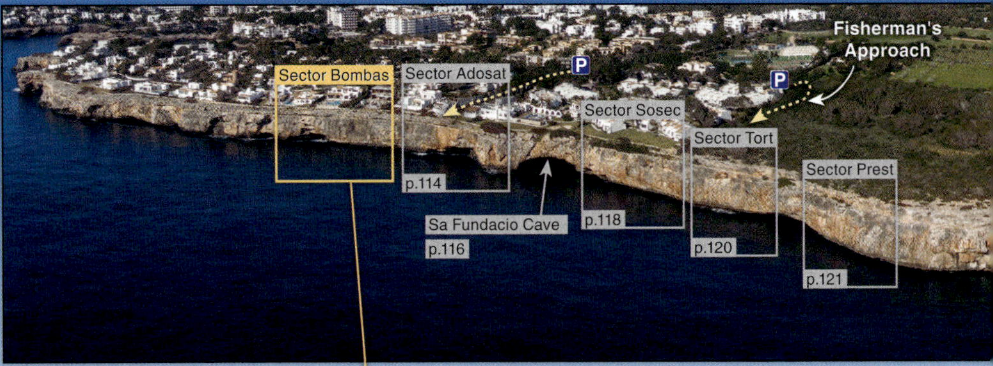

Cala Serena — Sector Bombas

Sector Bombas

The left side of Serena has some sharp and occasionally brittle rock. The further right you go the more things improve and the rock slowly turns to the more familiar golden pocketed walls.

Approach (map p.109) - For the first set of climbs (*Chanelance* to *Batalla de cazalla*) go 80m south beyond the main approach from the parking and make a rope-assisted descent. The rest of the routes are reached by rope-assisted descent and then a traverse leftwards.

Exits - Potential exit points are marked on the topo. Check them out before committing and remove all ropes when finished.

Descend to the left (looking in) of these climbs and traverse in.

❶	Chanelance	☼	6b SO
❷	Vacaciones en el mar		6c SO
❸	Mallorca es fonki		6c SO
❹	Escupe la flema	☼	6c SO
❺	Batalla de cazalla		6b SO

Sector Bombas **Cala Serena** *113*

- Serena Wall p.122
- Infinity Wall p.123
- Sector Tiramisu p.124
- Cala Mitjana p.96

16m

Rope-assisted descent

Exit

Descend to the right (looking in) of these climbs and traverse in.

6	Estilo Pancho Villa	2	6c *S0*
7	La escuela	2	6c *S0*
8	Zafarrancho		6c *S0*
9	Golpe bajo		6b *S0*
10	El mas fardon		6b *S0*
11	Tacon cubano		6b *S0*
12	Pasate el microfono		6b *S0*
13	Bombas		6b *S0*
14	Sifon y jena		6b *S0*
15	Don Simon		6b *S0*
16	La manicura		6b *S0*
17	La corna		6c *S0*
18	Cap torero sense banyas		6b *S0*
19	Guais estails		6b *S0*
20	Nora		6b *S0*

Cala Serena — Sector Adosat

Sector Adosat

This area has more golden pockets with mostly vertical and slabby walls found here except for lines emerging out of the caves.

Approach (map p.109) - The wall left of the large cave with the routes *Anselm* to *Efecto especial verbal I* is best reached by a rope-assisted descent, 20m south of the cave entrance. The cave approach used to be by a set of stairs away from the cliff edge although recent developments may restrict this. If accessible then squeeze through some bars and descend concrete stairs to sea level. Watch out for obstacles - a torch is useful but not essential. Failing this, an abseil to the right (looking in) is required.

Exits - Potential exit points are marked on the topo. Check them out before committing and remove all ropes when finished.

These climbs are reached by an descent line 20m south of the cave entrance.

❶ Anselm .... ☐ **6b** *S1*
❷ Especula .... ☐ **6b** *S1*
❸ Adosat .... ☐ **6b** *S1*
❹ Vuitmil .... ☐ **6b** *S1*
Jump off below the blank upper wall.

Sector Adosat — Cala Serena 115

The following set of routes are best reached through the cave if possible, or by abseil if this approach is not possible.

- **5 Efecto especial verbal I** .. 6b *S0*
  Jump off below the blank upper wall.
- **6 Toreros muertos I** 6b *S0*
  Jump off or continue up *Albornoz*.
- **7 Albornoz** .... 6b+ *S1*
- **8 Mocs i po** 6b *S1*
- **9 Moc** 6b *S2*
- **10 Efecto especial verbal II** 6b *S0*
- **11 Toreros muertos II** 6b *S0*
- **12 Mini me** 6b *S0*

Cala Serena — Sa Fundacio Cave

Sa Fundacio Cave

The Sa Fundacio Cave is often damp and many of the routes seldom dry out near the base.

Approach (map p.109) - The Sa Fundacio Cave is reached by walking directly to the cliff edge from the parking in front of the gated community and turning left onto the small headland.

Exits - It is essential to install your own exit rope before you start any climbing as it is impossible to exit the water without it in most cases. There are usually ropes dangling in the water along the cliff, but these can snap depending on the length of time they have been left in the sun for. Please remove your ropes after use.

① Diedre 1 .... 6b SO

② Sa fundacio .... 7a SO

③ Bou .... 7a SO
Rumour has it that this one climbs the roof of the cave, left to right, on big holds!

Pablo Escudero climbing the excellent *Redeemer* (6c) - *p.110* - at Sector Brazil.
Photo: Daimon Beail Collection

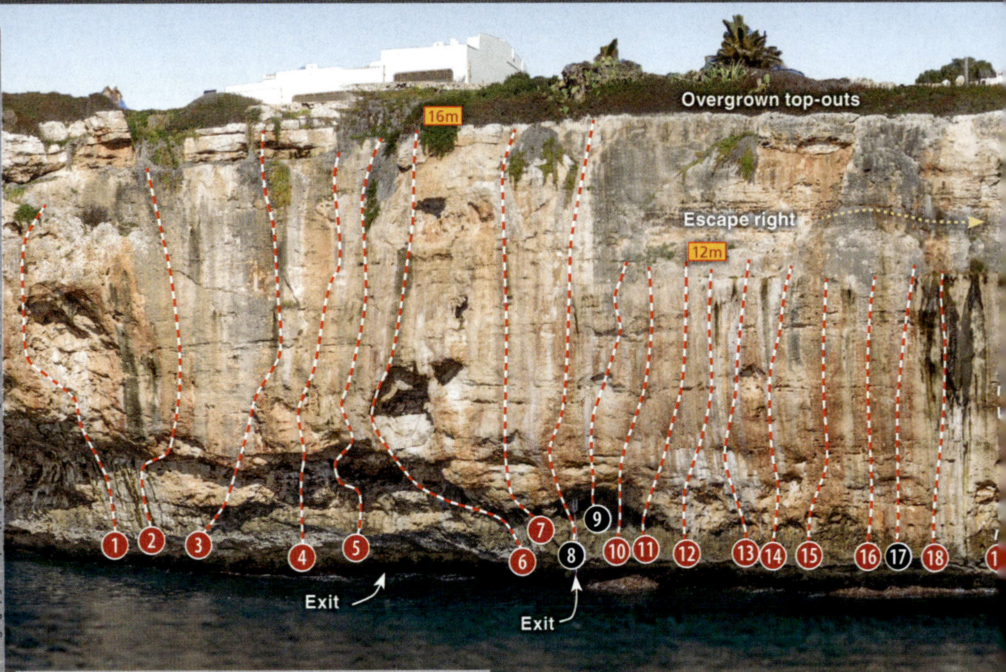

Cala Serena — Sector Sosec

Sector Sosec

The wall right of the Sa Fundacio Cave is a great area to get stuck into with many good routes. The climbing is on pocketed walls on the lower sections leading to technical and thin climbing on the upper walls. Most of the routes are accessed by *The Tortilla Traverse* which comes in from the right (looking in). The top-outs are overgrown for much of the area and it is advisable to traverse carefully rightwards when finishing the climbs. A rope placed down a certain section can speed things up and avoid the traverse right to get more done and conserve energy.

Approach (map and overview p.109) - Sector Sosec is reached by following the Fisherman's Approach to the cliff edge. The first eight routes, which are actually the right wall of the Sa Fundacio Cave, can be reached by *The Tortilla Traverse* or by abseil from above. A rope is advised to reach the base of the main Sosec descent.

Exits - It is vital you install your own exit rope before you start any climbing as it is impossible to exit the water without it in most cases. There are usually ropes dangling in the water along the cliff, but these can snap depending on the length of time they have been left in the sun for. Please remove your ropes after use.

① Vinga bou .... 6b *SO*

② Llet negra .... 7a *SO*

③ Aspergilo 6c *S1*

④ Manca .... 6c *SO*

⑤ Les ajudes .... 7a *SO*

⑥ Es pate .... 7a *SO*

⑦ Es bol.leti .... 6c *SO*

⑧ Es papa .... 7b *SO*

⑨ Medalles .... 7a+ *SO*

⑩ La xina .... 6c *SO*

⑪ Tokio .... 6b+ *SO*
Climb a steep wall to the vertical wall. Thin moves lead to a slopey finish. You can drift onto *Galactics* at the end which reduces the grade to **6b**.

⑫ Galactics .... 6b *SO*
Start just right of the cave.

⑬ Mega .... 6b *SO*

⑭ Setze jutges .... 6b *SO*

⑮ Mengen fetge .... 6b *SO*

⑯ Dolby .... 6b *SO*

⑰ Tot petit .... 7b *SO*

⑱ Pop .... 7a *SO*

Sector Sosec Cala Serena 119

19 Dreta 7a *S0*
20 Coloms 6a *S0*
21 Toques 6b *S0*
22 S'aixeta 7a *S0*
23 Down 6b *S0*
24 Alcaeda 7a *S0*
25 Ali muma ye 6c *S0*
26 Meteoro 6b *S0*
27 Nomas 6a *S0*
28 Aromes de Margrony 6a *S0*
Climb the right-hand side of the tufa.
29 Sóller 7a *S0*
Excellent technical climbing.
30 Es baluart .... 7a+ *S0*

31 Calvía .... 7a+ *S0*
32 Broker .... 6a+ *S0*
From a large bucket, use spaced holds to a thin upper wall.
33 Mapau .... 6a+ *S0*
A pocketed first half followed by an awesome 'crimp fest'.
34 Vip .... 6b+ *S0*
A little more taxing and committing than *Mapau*.
35 Rasputin 6a *S0*
Large pockets take you to the thin upper wall which has golden crimps everywhere.
36 Sosec .... 6a+ *S0*
Easy climbing to the groove on the left side of the block.
37 Mano negra 6b *S0*
Long moves to the lip and some powerful climbing above on sharp holds. *Photo p.107*.
38 The Tortilla Traverse .... 7a+ *S0*
80m+. Start at the bottom of the way down. Traverse all the way to finish up *Tokio*. Originally it went to *Vinga Bou* in the Sa Fundacio Area, but the caves are often wet making this difficult.
39 Bag Puss 6b *S1*
Straightforward climbing up a pocketed and crimpy wall. The angle eases the higher you get.
FA. James Cole 9.2006

Cala Serena — Sector Tort

Sector Tort

The shorter Tort Area routes all start off with wonderful holds but deliver you to blank upper section where many become unstuck. The climbs on the right of the wall can feel a bit high but the top sections tend to be easier than the beginnings. The cave climbs *Banyada* to *Submarina* need to have calm conditions since they can get very wet at the start - they may require a dry bag swim or boat support.

Approach (map p.109) - Sector Tort is reached by the Fisherman's Approach to the cliff edge. Then traverse right from the main Sosec descent line. It is also possible to make a higher diagonal descent.

Exits - It is vital you install your own exit rope before you start any climbing as it is impossible to exit the water without it in most cases. There are usually ropes dangling in the water along the cliff, but these can snap depending on the length of time they have been left in the sun for. Please remove your ropes after use.

① Romani 6a *S0*
② Dimiti 6a *S0*
③ Tort 6b *S0*
④ BBC 6b *S0*
⑤ Cantabrica 6b *S0*
⑥ Sa multa 6c *S0*
⑦ Espases 7a *S0*
A number of flowstone pockets and an awkward move out right lead to good edges. Thin side-pulls carry you to easier ground.
⑧ Terra 6b *S1*
Gymnastic moves off pockets lead to a short rest. Make some delicate moves out right and finish up the face.
⑨ Guantanamo 7b *S1*
⑩ Mi primera flinada 6b *S1*
An awesome route. Traverse to where the lower cave begins and head up some super slopers and side-pulls to reach the bulging upper wall. Power on to the top using some humongous and ever-so-slightly sharp jugs. *Photo p.125.*
⑪ Banyada 7b *S0*
⑫ Acuatic .... 7b+ *S0*
⑬ Abugraib .... 7b+ *S0*
⑭ Submarina .... 7b+ *S0*

Sector Prest — Cala Serena

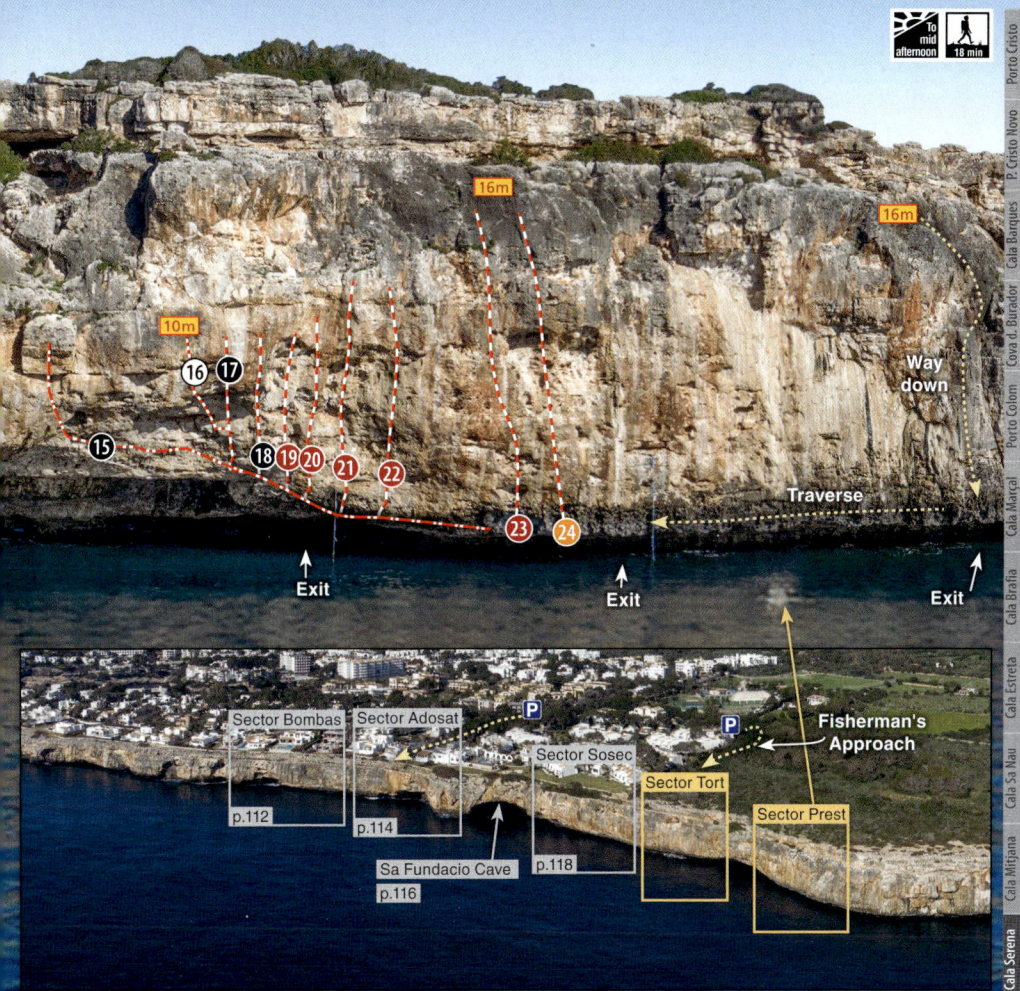

Sector Prest

The Prest Area feels slightly disconnected to the long wall to the left mainly due to the distant traverse back into the cave section. Climbs here are steep but often with good holds and very appealing to those after powerful steeper style climbs.

Approach (map p.109) - For Sector Prest, head north along the cliff edge. Descend easily on the right-hand wall and traverse leftwards to reach the climbs here.

Exits - It is vital you install your own exit rope before you start any climbing as it is impossible to exit the water without it in most cases. There are usually ropes dangling in the water along the cliff, but these can snap depending on the length of time they have been left in the sun. Please remove your ropes after use.

- ⑮ Es xirimollo ..... 7a+ SO
  A powerful and long traverse without many rests takes you into a steep and exhilarating finish.

- ⑯ Xapapote .... 8a SO
- ⑰ Superguapa .... 7b+ SO
- ⑱ Malle .... 7b+ SO
- ⑲ Diedre 2 .... 6c SO
- ⑳ Prest .... 6c SO
- ㉑ Gasolina .... 6b SO
- ㉒ Europa .... 6b SO
- ㉓ Sense casc .... 6b SO
- ㉔ Trobador .... 6a SO

Cala Serena — Serena Wall

Serena Wall

A fantastic wall with a striking leftward-slanting crack. The walls face east, getting a good dose of morning sun and benefitting from easterly winds to help keep things dry. Even in a damp state, they are all climbable in one way or another.

Approach (map and overview p.109) - From reaching the cliff edge via the Fisherman's approach, walk north until a high platform is visible below with a large boulder on top. Down-climb here to establish a base. From the platform, traverse right (looking in) and down a rightward-trending flake to good holds and easier ground. Head left along a narrow platform at half height and then down climb a small slab (installing a rope helps with this section) to a platform below. Traverse left from the platform onto *Squeeze* and *Sweet Serena*. Traverse right to reach *Pontas Revenge* and *Scrunch*.

Exits - Install a rope at the exit point marked.

❶ Squeeze .... 6b+ S0
From the cave, traverse left past *Sweet Serena* to a sequence of pockets. Climb these diagonally leftwards and up through a series of overlaps to reach a horizontal 'squeeze' finish.
FA. Bernard Exley 7.10.2012

❷ Sweet Serena 6b S0
Move leftwards from the ledge and down to reach a small cave. Chalk up and climb diagonally leftwards on jugs to reach the undercutting flake. Climb this to a corner and step left to finish up an easy-angled face.
FA. Daimon Beail 7.10.2012

❸ Pontas Revenge 5c S0
FA. Bernard Exley 7.10.2012

❹ Scrunch 6a S0
FA. Bernard Exley 13.10.2012

Infinity Wall Cala Serena

Infinity Wall

To the right of Serena Wall, Infinity Wall offers some good outings. The routes to the right-hand side of the cave are on a vertical wall so make sure you are able to push clear if coming off. The top-outs are slabby and make it easier to finish. The crag faces east, so catches the morning sun but does not suffer much from condensation because of the angle of the rock.

Approach (map and overview p.109) - From the large platform at the top of the crag, traverse right (looking in) and down a rightward-trending flake to good holds and easier territory. For the lines past *Stolen*, continue down and right to a large platform where an exit rope can be installed for the Infinity Wall area. Traverse rightwards to the cave mouth and continue on sharp holds to reach the other side and the lines there.

5 Lamancha .... 6a+ *S0*
Climb the line of weakness on the left side of the cave through a gap, and head onto the upper arete to then follow the grey streak to the top.
FA. Bernard Exley 13.10.2012

6 Lost in Lamancha 6b *S0*
Traverse onto the broken thread and up onto the ledge before moving left to join *Lamancha*. Break right again onto the steeper face and onto the easy-angled wall above.
FA. Daimon Beail 13.10.2012

7 Stolen 6a *S1*
Climb the bulging wall to a vertical face with some thin moves to reach the centre of the cave. Finish easily by climbing the left side of the cave.
FA. Bernard Exley 7.10.2012

8 To Infinity 6a *S1*
Climb directly to the right side of the cave and finish (after a short breather in the cave) on the right of the mouth.
FA. Daimon Beail 13.10.2012

9 Oceans in the Sky 6a *S1*
Lovely pocketed climbing keeping right of the smooth face. Proceed into the small recess and out on large holds.
FA. Daimon Beail 13.10.2012

10 Electric Sky 6a *S1*
Good climbing up the grey streak using some nicely placed cracks.
FA. Daimon Beail 13.10.2012

11 Prawn in the Sun 6a *S1*
The wall right of the large overhanging grey streak.
FA. Michal Becker 13.10.2012

12 Two Finger Fun 6a *S2*
A winding line across the face.
FA. Michal Becker 13.10.2012

Cala Serena — Sector Tiramisu

Sector Tiramisu

The right side of Serena has a good wall with a few offerings and plenty of potential. The crag faces east, so catches the morning sun.

Approach (map and overview p.109) - Continue north along the crag to reach the far right side of the crag. An abseil or rope-assisted descent is required if approaching *Tiramisu* directly. Alternatively you can traverse in from Infinity Wall area. The far end of the crag leads to the start of the traverse.

Exits - Install a rope at the exit point marked. For the traverse, identify the best location to support your needs.

Rope-assisted descent required or traverse in from Infinity Wall.

❶ Horizontal Shuffle — 6c+ SO
From the starting ledge, traverse rightwards with an initial crimpy section leading to better holds thereafter. Change direction and head up to easier climbing above.
FA. Henry Crawley 13.10.2015

❷ Tiramisu — 7a+ SO
Traverse right over the lower cave on good but spaced pockets to the large hole. Head straight up from here to eventually reach easier ground.
FA. Henry Crawley 13.10.2015

Down climb the right side of the crag.

❸ The Magic Bean Traverse — 6b SO
Start around the right side of the large arete (facing Cala Mitjana). Head down on some sharp rock and make a blind move around the arete onto a big ledge section. Clamber further down and left to a juggy break that leads under the lower roof section. The crux on the final section of the climb when heading up requires a big rockover to a jug on the slab.
FA. Henry Crawley, Gabriel Brigstow 11.10.2015

Delphine Byrne on the magnificent *Mi primera flinada* (6b) - *p.120* - at Sector Tort. This line has everything - tricky climbing lower down and an amazing juggy section higher up. One for everyone's ticklist! Photo: Beail Collection

Santanyí

Grade Spread | 1 | 9 | 5 | 2 | 5

Santanyí is a varied location. On the one hand you have the isolated and impressive arch of Es Pontas which is the location of one of the most famous and hardest deep water solos in the World - Chris Sharma's famous route also known as *Es Pontas*. Most of the climbs on the arch are hard although there are some which make for fun outings.

The other aspect of DWS at Santanyí is a complete contrast - a friendly holiday DWS venue with a glorious (though popular) beach, turquoise sea glistening in the sun and some short, have-a-go, deep water solos to enjoy. The nearby presence of the sport climbing cliffs of Tijuana means you can mix and match your climbing needs and enjoy both disciplines. Although the number of DWS routes in the bay area is limited, the routes are great fun, especially *Super Sonic*. The rock is a little bit brittle in places and the far back section of 'the cove' is shallow. A boat is useful though not essential if you want to commute to the different crags more quickly.

Santanyí

Toni Lamprecht, one of the early pioneers of deep water soloing on the island, climbing one of the most iconic deep water solos on the planet, Chris Sharma's *Es Pontas* (9a+) - *p.131* - on the Es Pontas arch at Santanyí. Photo: Rasmus Kaessmann

Conditions

Treasure Island - Needs a nice calm day as it requires a swim to get to, but the traverse often stays dry and chalk is not essential.
Es Pontas - A reasonably calm day is needed to get to the arch. Best conditions for the steep moves under arch are cooler air and a light breeze as it can get greasy otherwise.
Bay Area - The bay is relatively sheltered. Care is needed if using a boat to reach the crag from across the bay since other boats and small sailing yachts sometimes visit the area. *Super Sonic* can get greasy, but the other lines often stay in relatively good condition.

Santanyí

Approaches

From the outskirts of Santanyí, follow signs for Cala Figuera and Cala Santanyí and continue for around 2km to a roundabout.

For Es Pontas - From the roundabout, turn right signed to Cala Santanyí and Platja. After 1km, turn right at a small roundabout and follow the road up and around above the beach until a crossroads after about 1km. Park here and walk south up a road marked with a no entry sign. Turn right, then left and then right again as the road turns into a track. Follow the track and a well trodden path, past a large Totum rock statue, down to the cliff edge and a viewpoint overlooking the Es Pontas arch. See crag approach pages from here.

For cliff-top parking for the Bay Area - From the roundabout, go straight on, signed Cala Figuera. About 200m after the roundabout, bear right - this time signed to Cala Santanyí. Take the first left (signed to Cala Figuera) and then the first right (signed 'DRAC'). Continue along this road, to a small traffic island. Park around here carefully as it is a residential area and walk past a barrier in the road to a tower on the clifftop. Follow the cliff-edge path rightwards (looking out) until the path drops down to the base of the crag. Turn right to reach the Bay or left to the Tijuana sport climbing.

For beach parking for the Bay Area - A good option if only doing DWS is to approach from the beach. From the roundabout, turn right signed to Cala Santanyí and Platja. Follow the signs to Platja down to a car park down at the beach. From here it is possible to walk up the left or right side of the bay to reach the climbing areas.

Treasure Island

There is a long traverse on the section of cliff between Es Pontas and small bay east of it.
Approach - Walk down to the furthest point east on the cliff edge to reach the water and swim across the cove.
Exit - These can be located as you traverse.

❶ Treasure Island   **6b** *S1*
100m+ Follow the easiest line across to the next bay. Make your way back over the top down to the start and swim back to base.
FA. Daimon Beall 10.2004

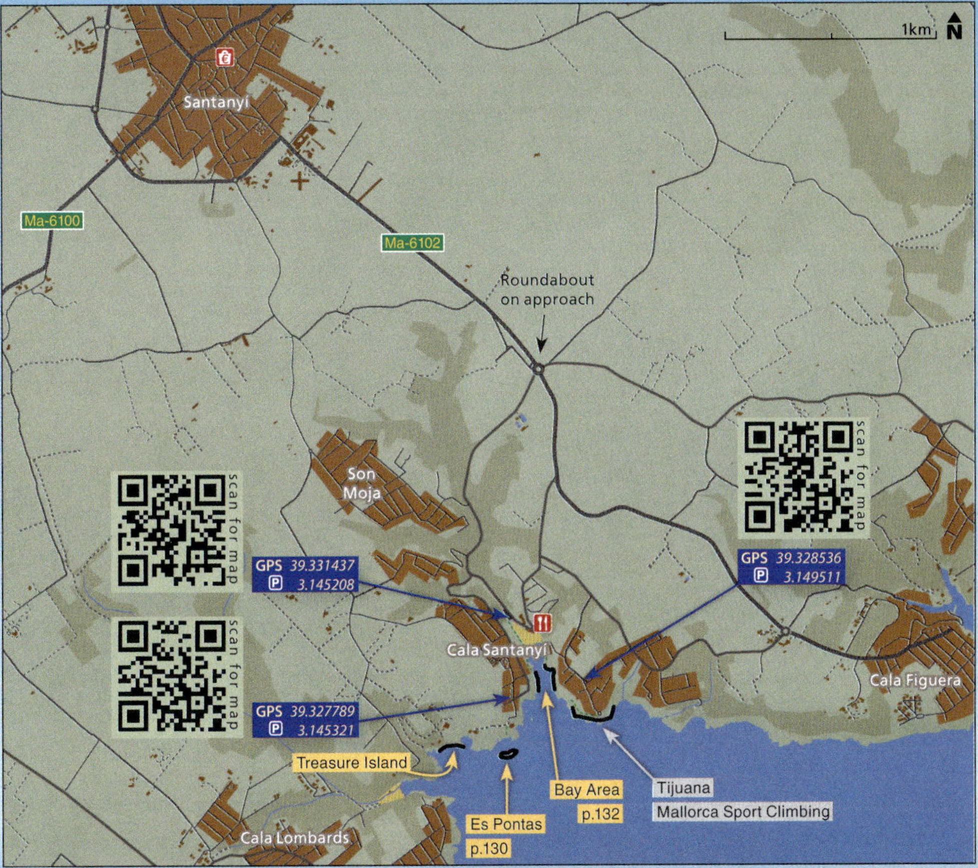

Santanyí 129

Santanyí — Es Pontas

Es Pontas

This magnificent arch is for the elite climbers and home to one of the most famous DWS routes on the planet named after the arch its self - *Es Pontas*. This major route has a number of top standard but relatively easier variations. For those not up to these grades, a lot of fun can be had by traversing either leg of the arch or by climbing the nose to the top to embrace the elite climber's podium at the top.

Approach (map and overview p.129) - From the viewing area, walk right (looking out) along the cliff for 50m to where you can climb down to a large platform. Gear up and head back left (looking out) under the cliff to the closest point to the arch. The crossing is a shallow section of water which has boulders under foot. Most people swim across with a dry bag or use an inflatable boat. In rough seas, take extreme caution as one or two obstacles are hidden along the way. Traverse right to reach the main routes. There is an easy way up and down on the west nose of the arch.

Exit - Take a rope and an inflatable boat to help you exit from the water.

1 Pontas Traverse 6c S0
A tricky traverse around the west pillar.

2 Southwest Face .... 6a+ S1
Up the centre of the technical face.
FA. James Cole 2004

3 Dihedral .... 6a+ S2
Not too bad to climb but much harder (6c) to get to.

4 Baby Sepia .... 7b+ S2
A sneaky but exciting outing up the left-hand side of the arch. Either climb up (or reverse down) *Dihedral*, then pull round onto the face. Relatively easy pickings for this arch.
FA. Toni Lamprecht 2005

Es Pontas **Santanyí** *131*

⑤ Es Pontas .... 9a+ S2
Start at the base of the pillar on a small ledge about 2m above the water. Tackle a boulder problem over a small roof and onto the overhanging face to reach some slightly better holds. Continue for about 15 more moves using a series of pinches, pockets and the odd tufa before moving right into the barrel of the gun. Take on a huge dynamic lunge (has been done static) from two undercuts to a large and hard-to-stick pocket. From the pocket, continue rightwards via a series of edges leading to the arete on the landward side of the arch. Follow some small sloping holds on the arete until you reach the central point of the arch. Power on to the top to join the best climbers in the world.
Photo p.126.
FA. Chris Sharma 26.9.2006

⑥ Pontasaffair .... 8b+ S2
A fine addition to the Pontas family which takes in the arch experience but at a slightly lesser grade. Start as for *Es Pontas* and make your way to the launching holds on the famous dyno. Continue, moving slightly leftwards to avoid the dyno, heading straight up towards the lip to finish on the wall above.
FA. Toni Lamprecht 3.10.2008

⑦ Pontasaffair - Alt 8c S2
An alternative harder finish to *Pontasaffair* that links *Pontasaffair* into the final moves of *Pontax*.
FA. Toni Lamprecht 3.10.2008

⑧ Pontax 8c S2
After the dyno on *Es Pontas*, continue up for another 6m on a series of finger pockets to top out on the seaward side.
FA. Chris Sharma 11.2005

⑨ Minitas .... 8a+ S2
Starting from the right-hand side of the arch, make your way over to the dyno holds on *Es Pontas*. Move left, (avoiding the dyno) and continue up leftwards to finish on the final moves of *Baby Sepia*.
FA. Chris Sharma 2005

⑩ Stop Look and Listen .... 6a+ S2
A pleasant anti-clockwise tour of the east pillar.
FA. Daimon Beail 10.2003

⑪ Pontification 6a S0
On the seaward side of the east pillar, climb the middle right side of the blank-looking wall on crimps and slots and pull onto the easier-angled ground.
FA. Dan Webber 23.9.2009

Santanyí — Bay Area - Super Sonic

Bay Area - Super Sonic

A small area with some well-positioned traverses above a deep undercut cave. It gets the morning sun and is located on the far side of the bay.

Approach (map p.129) - Walk up the right side of the bay from the beach. Alternatively a water crossing is required.

❶ Man of Steel .... 6a+ S0
A short pocketed traverse on the left side of the cave.
FA. Oli Mittins 16.8.2016

❷ Super Sonic .... 6c+ S0
Climb out across the lip of the cave on good holds until almost one third of the way across. Climb diagonally up from there.
FA. Daimon Beail 10.2003

❸ Bird Watching 6b S0
From the platform, climb the flake and then traverse the break-line to the other platform.
FA. Julian Chapman 10.2003

❹ Bird Watching Direct 5a S0
An early exit from *Bird Watching*.
FA. Julian Chapman 10.2003

Bay Area - The Cove — Santanyí

Bay Area - The Cove
A small area with some shorter routes. It gets the afternoon sun.

Approach (map p.129) - Approach from the clifftop parking for Tijuana sport crag, or by walking from the beach parking. The routes are mostly approached from a slightly submerged platform. This can be reached by swimming or down climbing *Naked Germans*. *Mr. Smith* is gained down the right side of The Cove.

5 Cocktail O'Clock 7a S2
Use two pockets in the left edge of the roof to tackle the bulge. Keep left of the flat boulder (2m deep to the right) at all times.
FA. Davy Vos 15.9.2015

6 Naked Germans 4c S0
A good descent route.
FA. Daimon Beail 10.2003

7 Wave Machine 5c S0
Traversing right into The Cove leads to a slightly steeper wall. Climb up just right of the arete and past the left side of the lip.
FA. Daimon Beail 10.2003

8 Vino Master 6a S0
Climb up to and over the right side of the lip. Be careful as it's a bit loose at the top.
FA. Julian Chapman 10.2003

9 Without a Paddle .... 7a+ S1
Start from the jug close to the water, head up to a sloping ledge and follow the crack-line right to crimpy moves and jug. Keep an eye on the water depth below.

10 Mr. Smith 6a S2
It gets very shallow towards the back of the cave, which is where you should really finish.
FA. Steve Smith 10.2003

Cala Llombards

Cala Lombards is one of the more esoteric venues on the island. The fact that it is mostly hard climbs up to 17m in height keeps most people away! It is split into two areas. Llombards East, the closest of the two, has the most routes with a wider grade range. Llombards West takes a lot of dedication to reach, involving a long adventurous scramble along a narrow ledge. The crag is famous primarily for Miquel Riera's *Follam Balam* which is a superb but rarely repeated roof climb with a famous no-hands rest.

Conditions

Cave venues almost always have some form of greasy rock within them, but these crags are more exposed to the ocean winds which helps keep the moisture build-up to a minimum. The top-outs to some of the lines are a little bit friable in places.

The late Miquel Riera, who began unearthing deep water soloing back in the late 70s and became the island's ambassador for the sport. He brought climbers from across the globe to help contribute to the development and developed many areas of his own. Here Miquel is on his mega route *Follam Balam* (8a+) - *p.138* - in the cave at Llombards East. Photo: Rasmus Kaessmann

Cala Llombards

Approach
From Santanyí, follow signs for Es Llombards on the Ma-6100 to a large roundabout. Take the second exit to Cala Llombards and continue for about 3km until you reach a built-up area. Take the second left turn signed to Platja shortly after the mini roundabout. Follow this and take the first right. Drive down to where the road curves left and then branch right. Shortly after there is a road to your right with a no entry sign. Park considerately in the area before the sign and walk down this road to a turning circle. Follow some stairs down to the reach the cliff edge and a small headland.

Llombards West - turn right (looking out) and cross the rocky cliff edge until you reach the large bay. Continue adventurously along the mid-height ledge to reach the crag on the other side.

Llombards East - turn left (looking out) and make a tricky traverse along the narrow mid-height ledge to reach the crag.

GPS 39.317262 / 3.135629

Llombards West **Cala Llombards** 137

Llombards West

An isolated spectacular crag with some high routes. It sees few visits.

Approach - Head right (looking out) along the cliff edge, past some large boulders which block the path. A rope is needed to descend to the base of the crag.

Exit - Install a rope on the exit point before you set off.

❶ **Sa tangent**............. 13 🧗 ☐ 6c S1
The easiest of the three gets trickier near the top.
FA. Miquel Riera 2006

❷ **Locat matador**.... 13 🧗 ☐ 7c S1
Follow *Sa tangent* to the lip of the cave and move out right to a block at the base of a flake. Climb this and the shallow groove above with care.
FA. Miquel Riera, Chris Sharma 2006

❸ **Esplendor geometrico**... 23 🧗 ☐ 8a+ S1
The big daddy of this wall. From where *Locat matador* launches up the block, continue to the arete and navigate your way on the steep underside of the face. Pull round slightly left near the top to make the final moves to victory.
FA. Miquel Riera 2006

Cala Llombards — Llombards East

Llombards East

The East area is more extensive and has one outstanding classic hard line. There are a few quality easier routes too, though these are quite high. The crag is exposed to the sun although the cave routes may get shade due to steepness.

Approach (map and overview p.136) - Walk left (looking out) and make your way along a small ledge, past some pinch points along the way, until you are above the cave. Reaching the start of *Follam Balam* requires a dinghy. Use the water access point located on the headland.

Exit - A natural exit is possible on the left-hand side of the cave (looking in). It is also possible to install a rope to exit on the right-hand side of the cave. There is also an exit point within the cave.

❶ **Sa rossaguera** 6a S0
From just above sea level, climb easily to the top.
FA. Miquel Riera 2006

❷ **Aresta** 6b S0
Climb the left side of the arete around the mouth of the cave.
FA. Miquel Riera 2006

③ **Follam Balam** .... 8a+ S0
Seldom repeated but certainly the classic of the crag! A boat is required to get to the start. Navigate your way over the long roof to join *Balam*. There is a no-hands rest near the lip of the cave, so take full advantage of it. The final section is the crux and quite thin and technical. *Photo p.134*.
FA. Miquel Riera 2006

Llombards East Cala Llombards

④ Te lo juro por Snoopy .... 8a+ S0
A harder and more direct finish to *Balam*.
FA. Chris Sharma 2006

⑤ Balam 8a S0
From the ledge at half height, launch across the roof and power your way up and right on good holds to the upper wall. More technical face climbing awaits before the top.
FA. Miquel Riera 2006

⑥ Lama 7b S1
A short face climb on the right-hand side of the cave.
FA. David Lama 2006

⑦ Spider Salad 6b S0
A short problem up the left side of the bulge.
FA. Miquel Riera 2006

⑧ Spiders with Chips 6b S0
A short problem up the right side of the bulge.
FA. Miquel Riera 2006

Sa Calobra

Grade Spread | - | 4 | 6 | 1 | -

Sa Calobra takes effort to get to but, if the conditions are good, it is an amazing spot to visit, even if only for a rest day. The climbing is located on the walls around the exit gorge from the Torrent de Pareis which can be a fast flowing river in the winter months or after heavy rain. Normally the river is dry and the mouth of the gorge is just a pebble-beach that slopes sharply into the sea. The area is usually very busy with coach loads of visitors and this means your climbing activities become the centre of attention especially if you climb on the Arena Wall. A boat is recommended since one or two of the routes are difficult to access and get to, especially *The Mallorcan* which also has a long swim back to shore.

Conditions

Since Sa Calobra is on the edge of the mountain range it attracts more changeable weather. This is less of a problem in June but in mid-October you may get rained off. The cove faces northwest, and because of the steepness of the surrounding cliffs and mountains, the sun normally hits the area from midday to early afternoon.

Sa Calobra 141

Approach

Sa Calobra is on the north side of the island and needs to be approached from the scenic Ma-10 road. This can be gained from Sóller, Inca-Lluc or Pollença. The turn-off to Sa Calobra is well signed at a busy junction with a restaurant and distinct disused bridge over the road. Descend the rollercoaster road down the mountain praying you aren't behind a very slow coach. Just before the tiny village at the bottom is a pay and display car park on the right. From here, walk down to the seafront and turn right. Follow the path along the front until you come to a series of small, well-lit tunnels. Squeeze your way through them, to emerge at the other side and the mouth of the Torrent de Pareis.

An alternative fun (but more costly) method of getting to Sa Calobra is to take the tourist boat from Port de Sóller. It is a scenic 60-minute ride each way.

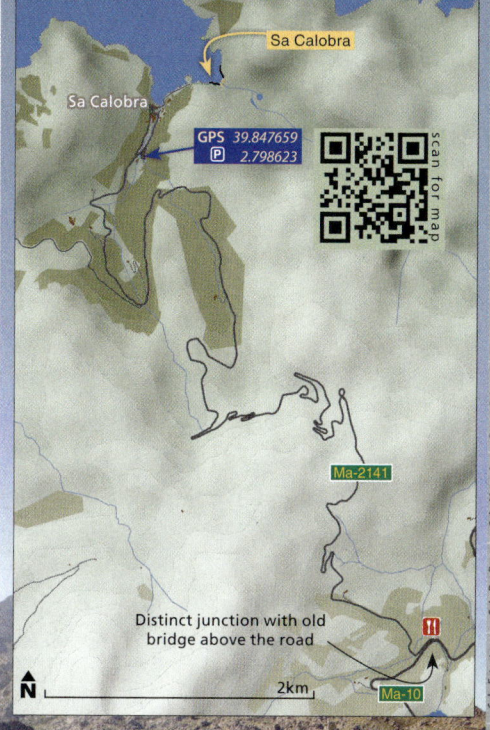

Sa Calobra — The Professor Wall

The Professor Wall
The east wall of the mouth of the gorge has a selection of traverses and a magnificent tufa-covered wall out of sight of the beach. A boat is useful to get to the starts. It is west facing but gets the shade early due to the surrounding walls.

Approach (map and overview p.141) - Start on the beach reached through the tunnels.
Exit - Swim or, better, boat back to the beach.

❶ The Mallorcan 7a S0
This route is out of sight on a tufa-covered wall. Gain the base of the longest tufa by boat and follow it via a lovely jug to where the tufa fattens. Navigate around the right side of this and head up onto the slab to the right-hand exit. Be careful with your boat at the start since the sharp rock has been know to puncture flimsy inflatables.
FA. Ged Desforges 9.2007

❷ The Little Professor 5c S0
60m+. The long traverse on the right-hand wall. Swim or boat out about 10m and pull out of the water at the first clear exit point on the wall. Traverse at any height, making it whatever grade you like, **5c** is average. A boat is advised for the return, and in case you fall, since it is a long swim. Alternatively, you can reverse it.
FA. Daimon Beail, S.Smith, J.Chapman 30.9.2003

❸ The Mad Professor .... 6c+ S0
From the start of *The Little Professor*, head right on fantastic rock to a tricky handrail and a slap for a large bucket. Continue as far as you can and bail out just before the shallow water and the end of *Eatsy's Cave*.
FA. Daimon Beail 17.6.2005

❹ Eatsy's Cave .... 6b+ S3
From the beach, traverse leftwards above shallow water on a ledge until you're sitting in the cave. Use a huge pocket to work your way out of the cave to the headwall above. Very shallow water so take extra care. Swim back or extend into *The Mad Professor* and *The Little Professor* for a mega tick!
FA. Rob Heirene, Tomas Pupsys 12.10.2013

← Exit

Boat — Swim or boat — Beach

The Mouth

The mouth of the gorge makes a spectacular setting and the west wall has some fun little climbs to explore.

Approach (map and overview p.141) - For the first route, start on the beach reached through the tunnels. For the other two, either swim from the beach, or discreetly walk around the no entry sign on the tunnel path and cross a railing to gain the steps.

Exit - Swim back to the beach or pull out onto the steps.

5 Left Side Traverse 5c S2
Depending on the sea conditions, either wade or swim out (creating different starting points) and pull on and out of the water on jugs. Traverse right (watching the depth at the start) at various heights and finish by jumping off just as you get to the blank orange wall. (The next two climbs start over on the right side of this.) Swim back to shore. The continuation across this wall to the steps has not yet been climbed.
FA. Sarp Akcay 16.10.2022

6 Water Logged 6a S0
Pull out of the water and follow the big flake up and right. At the top of the flake, climb up to the sloping ledge. A variation of it can be done from the steps missing the first section. Climb down the diagonal ledge to finish.
FA. Julian Chapman 30.9.2003

7 Sa Pose .... 6b+ S0
A powerful traverse. Follow the faint crack from the massive flake on positive holds to big side-pulls. Power upwards to a ledge. Work your way down the ledge and back to the start.
FA. Daimon Beail 30.9.2003

Sa Calobra — The Arena

The Arena

The Arena is the first area you reach before entering the tunnels. It is named because it has a viewing gallery and you will become the centre of attention if climbing here. All the routes require a jump descent to get off.

Approach (map and overview p.141) - Approach from a rocky platform just over the left side of the railing, and descend from here.

Exit - In calm seas exiting is extremely easy as there is an underwater ledge at the bottom of the natural descent line into the sea. In slightly rougher conditions a rope would be useful. Also climb with care at the bottom, as it is normally quite slippery and wet.

❶ The Fulcher .... 6b+ SO
A fantastic line to a big descent jump. Traverse the handrail along and down past the arete of *Wax* until you reach a crouching position under a crack-line. Follow this until you can finish in a recess. Jump off.
FA. Daimon Beall 17.6.2005

❷ The Felcher .... 6a+ SO
Start up the crack behind the arete and pull into the corner. A hard move using an undercut and a small pocket enables you to reach a tufa pinch. From there, use crimps on the face to reach good pockets and the alcove right of *The Fulcher*.
FA. Bernard Exley 2011

❸ Wax .... 7a SO
A stunning find. Traverse the handrail until you reach the arete. Climb the right-hand side of it making some technical moves to a jug. Continue to wind your way up the face to pockets out left. Jump from here.
Photo opposite.
FA. James Cole 17.6.2005

❹ The Exhibitionist Finish .. 7a+ SO
Exit *Wax* midway and climb diagonally up to the recess via a blind crimp and some sloping holds.
FA. Chris Hudgins 18.9.2015

Adam Brown climbing *Wax* (7a) - *opposite* - located in The Arena area of Sa Calobra. This climb catches the attention of tourists passing by and is set in an incredible location. This makes it very memorable indeed, especially if the encouragement is anything like it was on the first ascent back in 2005. Photo: Beall Collection

Port de Sóller

Grade Spread | 3 | 3 | 13 | 2 | -

Port de Sóller is well known for its sport climbing but it also has some good deep water soloing venues. The Bay Area offers a series of quality sectors connected by approach traverses. It has plenty to offer the mid-grade soloist and is easy to get to. To the north of the sport climbing crag known as Port de Sóller is the isolated Cova de ses Puntes. First discovered by Miquel Riera and Toni Josep, this steep cave has a handful of quality routes that reach around 12m in height. A third venue called Cap Gros is situated out on the east headland and consists of a huge 40m cliff with super-hard routes with crux moves at around the 20m mark. These are mostly the work of Chris Sharma. The crag is only accessible by boat and the routes are not documented in detail here.

Approach

Bay Area - From Sóller continue to follow signs to Port de Sóller along the MA-11. Just before you reach the Port de Sóller tunnel, branch right (signed 'Port de Sóller', 'en Repic'). After 400m take the first left turn across the tramway, discreetly signed to Platja d'en Repic. This road winds down to behind the sea front buildings bearing left to a large car park. From here, walk between the buildings to the sea front. Make your way along the water's edge until it gets rocky, then follow a path along a disused pipe covered in concrete. Continue as far as you can onto the rocks which veer to the left. Keep going and traverse a large dusty rock pillar rightwards, then squeeze through the centre of it to get to the other side (rock shoes needed). Continue along the rocky platforms until you can launch your dinghy or tackle the *Aqua Phobia* traverse.

Cova de ses Puntes - Drive to Port de Sóller through the tunnel on the Ma-11. At the roundabout, take the second exit and turn right at the next T-junction. Continue straight up the hill for about 400m to where the road turns sharply back left. Continue straight past the blue dead end sign and wind your way uphill for another 400m or so (take advantage of any parking spots on this stretch of road but don't block passing places). At the point where the road turns sharply right, two large gates are visible on the left corner. Squeeze through the gap (steps in wall with the words 'Torre' written on the post) to reach an open area with a number of paths running from it. Follow the path almost directly ahead of you as it disappears down into the undergrowth. Continue down the right-hand side of a narrow gully and down the hill into woodland. Head left at the point where the path splits, to eventually reach the dry riverbed which leads to the sea. Head along the left side of the small inlet and up onto the cliff edge (over the mound) where Cova de Ses Puntes can be found.

Tom Le Fanu on his route *Linquine* (7a) - *p.151* - on the Aqua Wall at Port de Sóller. Photo: Beail Collection

Port de Sóller — Cova de ses Puntes

Cova de ses Puntes
An isolated and exceptionally atmospheric cave.

Approach (map p.146) - The first two lines are approached from the left-hand descent. The remaining lines are reached from the right-hand descent with a large ledge to chalk up from.

Exits - Exit is possible from either side of the cave in calm seas, but take an extra rope just in case.

Conditions - The cave faces northwest and does not see any direct sun until the evening. It is also rather exposed to the elements and needs a calm day for a visit and a light northwesterly breeze to dry things out.

❶ Supermanolo — 6b SO
Start from the left side of the cave mouth and climb the lip of the cave until you reach easier ground above.

❷ Republica Sinestra — 7c SO
Traverse right into the cave for a few metres before launching up the steep wall and out over the lip.

❸ Cristo — 7a SO
From the right side of the cave, traverse left into the centre and onto the bulging wall to start. Continue traversing left across and up into the back of the cave (often wet) to reach a recess and crack-line which leads to easier ground.

Cova de ses Puntes — Port de Sóller

4 **PSM**.................. 6c S0
Climb the centre of the cave, which is crimpier than the rest.

5 **Metxicans** 6c S0
Just right of centre is a small in-cut hole. Climb left over this and up to join the remainder of *Tanassa*.

6 **Tanassa** 6b S0
Just to the right of *Metxicans* is an easier but ever so slightly steeper wall. The large holds keep this line in check!

7 **Tramontana**........... 6c S1
The right-hand side of the cave. Watch the ledge at the start.

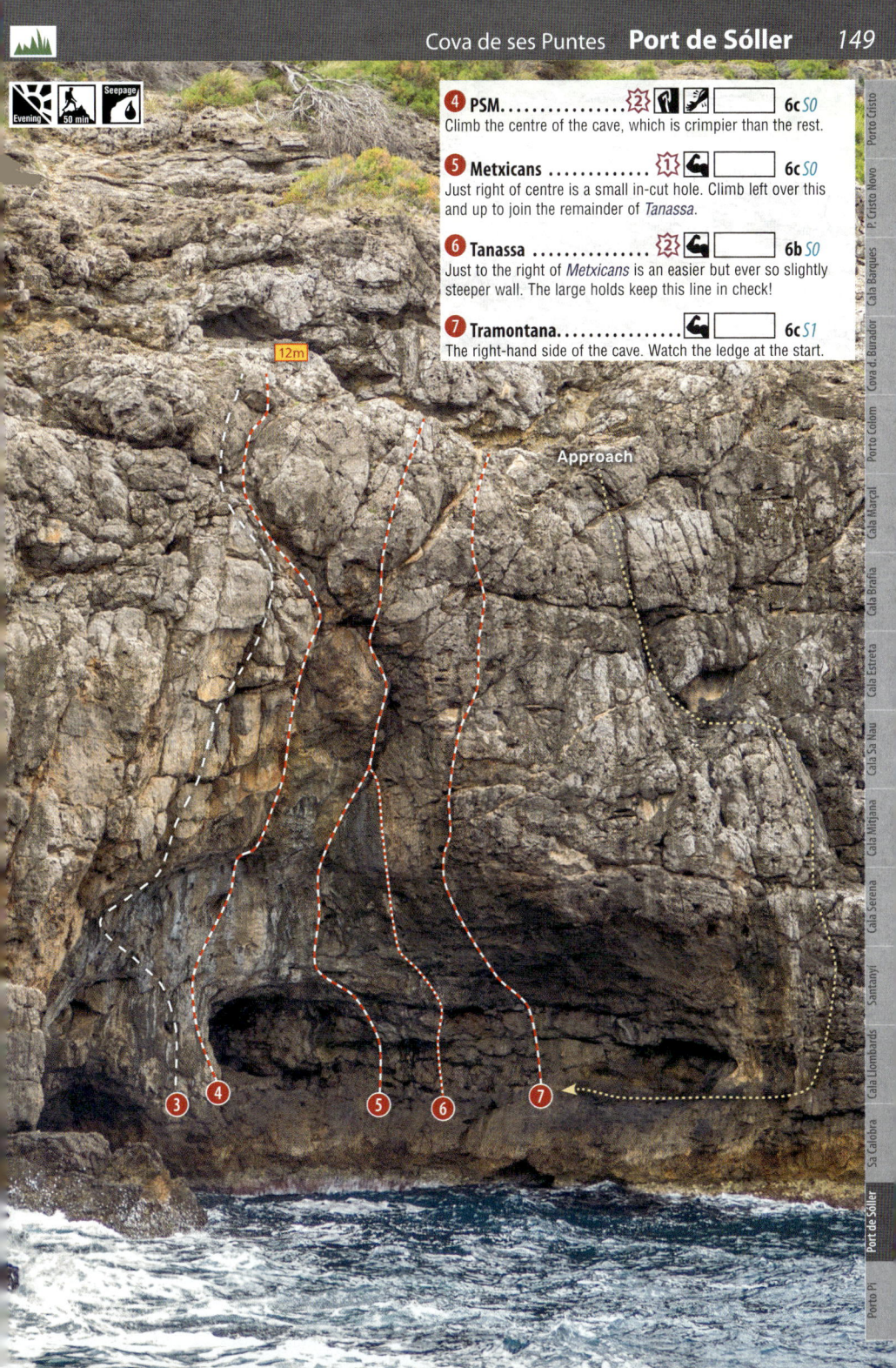

Port de Sóller — Bay Wall

Bay Wall

The crags in the Bay Area face east so generally only get the morning sun. The walls are sheltered, and can prevent the wind from drying the rock quickly.
Approach (map p.146) - *Aqua Phobia* starts from the rocky platform in the corner of the bay. *Michalien* launches out from *Aqua Phobia*.
Descent - For *Michalien*, head down to the left and then back into *Aqua Phobia*.

❶ **Aqua Phobia** .... 6b+ *S0*
An excellent traverse normally started from the far side of the bay and climbed left to right, with one of the trickier section is near the end. If starting from the landing platform and traversing from right to left, make your way under the shelf, then up and left using a big thread to help you.
FA. Daimon Beail 28.9.2003

❷ **Michalien** 4a *S1*
Midway through *Aqua Phobia* is a flat-looking wall. Climb the left side of this using the ramp for the left hand. Finish up the cracks above.
FA. Michal Becker 6.10.2010

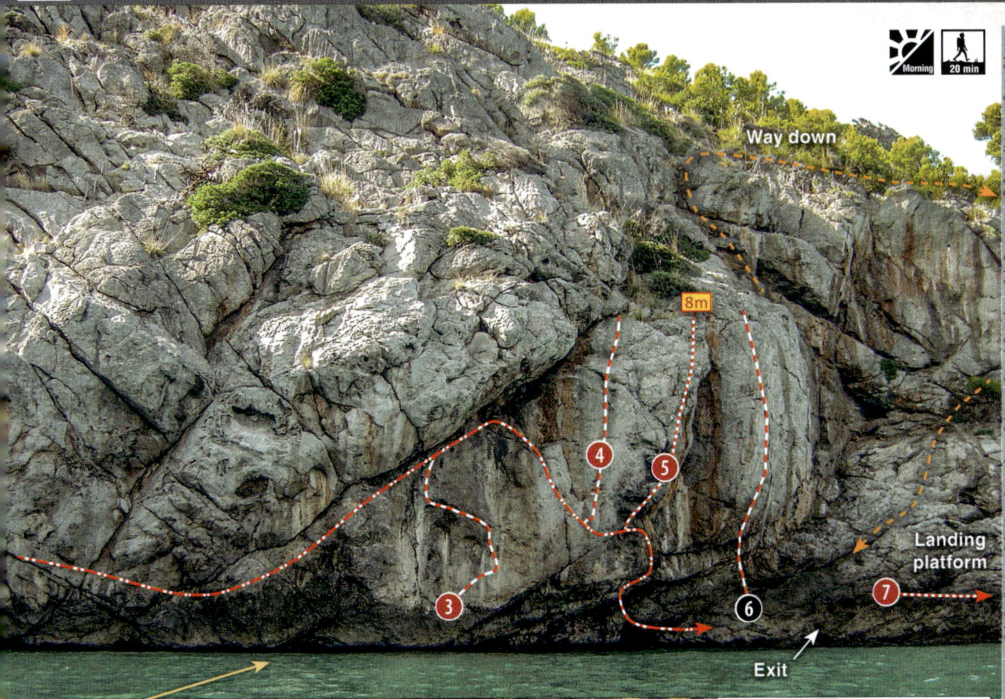

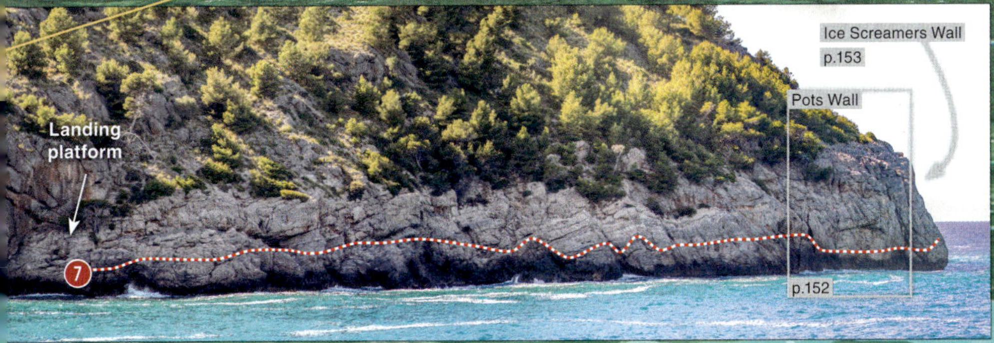

Aqua Wall — Port de Sóller

Aqua Wall

Approach (map p.146) - This wall is best approached along *Aqua Phobia* or by boat (which is required for *Alex*'s). There is an approach from the road above but this is hard to find, overgrown and not recommended.
Descent - Clamber over the top and back to the landing platform or carefully jump off into the sea.

❸ Alex's 6b S0
From a boat, locate a thin ledge and perch under the wall just right of the crack. Traverse up and right to a deep pocket and then back left and up to rejoin *Aqua Phobia*.
FA. Alex Barrett 31.8.2024

❹ Linguine 7a S0
Reverse *Aqua Phobia* to the left side of the arete and climb the face. *Photo p.147*.
FA. Tom Le Fanu 6.10.2010

❺ The Little Blue .... 6b+ S0
Reverse *Aqua Phobia* to the left side of the arete then make your way up the arete on jugs. 6b+ for the start, the rest is only 4a.
FA. Daimon Beail 28.9.2003

❻ It Tastes Like the Sea 7b S2
The blank arete. Hard and crimpy climbing all the way.
FA. Steve Smith 28.9.2003

❼ Little Princess .... 6b+ S0
An adventurous left-to-right traverse from the landing platform to the far end of the crag. If done low, it provides some interesting climbing. Finish up *Big Easy Flake - p.153*. The harder bits can normally be bypassed higher up.
FA. Daimon Beail 28.9.2003

Port de Sóller — Pots Wall

Pots Wall

Approach (map p.146, overview p.150) - Approach by traversing *Little Princess* from the platform. Alternatively, walk above the crag along some platforms with sections of scramble, then reverse down to gain the traverse. Alternatively, use a boat since it is quite easy to get onto land in this area.

① A Passage to the New 6a S1
Follow the rampline to the roof and climb the right-hand side to the top.
FA. Daimon Beail 28.9.2003

② Pots 6b S0
Follow the crack-line under the ramp to the roof and finish as for *A Passage to the New*.
FA. Steve Smith 28.9.2003

③ Squid 6b S0
Start below a flake and climb this to join and finish up *A Passage to the New*.
FA. Daimon Beail 28.9.2003

④ Dim Dim 5a S0
Climb the wall right of the face that bulges slightly over the water and veers left at the top.
FA. Daimon Beail 28.9.2003

Ice Screamers Wall — Port de Sóller

Ice Screamers Wall
Named after the impressive project up the centre of the wall which is still unclimbed after more than 20 years, dubbed *Ice Screamers*. At the moment it has a trio of easier routes which require a traverse approach.
Approach (map p.146, overview p.150) - Follow *Little Princess* or walk over the top and down climb *The Ease of Passage*, or the ramp to its left (looking in) to gain the traverse line.

5 The Ease of Passage 3a S3
The easy way up, or down. Can be approached along *Little Princess* with no increase in grade.
FA. Daimon Beail 28.9.2003

6 Deep Sea Climbing 5c S1
There are plenty of little lines but the route up the stuck-on flake is the nicest. Can be approached along *Little Princess* with no increase in grade.
FA. Daimon Beail 28.9.2003

7 Big Easy Flake 4a S2
The finish to *Little Princess* that requires a little bit of care near the top. The traverse onto this wall is harder than the climb itself. It can be tackled as an isolated climb if you paddle out and pull on from the water - it is S2 so take care.
FA. Daimon Beail 28.9.2003

Porto Pi

| Grade Spread | – | 5 | 4 | 1 | 1 |

Porto Pi is a great little venue near the Palma docks and is convenient for some first or last day soloing in relation to your flight, or are local to the area. Porto Pi is also where deep water soloing in Mallorca began back in 1978, when a young Miquel Riera first began exploring the possibility of climbing above deep water.

Approach
From the city of Palma, travel along the Ma-1 until you come to an area called Porto Pi. Look out for the shopping mall with a huge 'Porto Pi' sign on it. Navigate the outer roundabout and head south signed to 'Dic de l'Oest' (Western Port) for around 400m until you see a big parking area on the right. Park here and it is a two-minute walk to the crag below.

Conditions
The rock is soft and brittle in places and a little loose near the top, so take care in places. Also, watch out for the accumulation of rubbish in the sea, which sometimes happens around mid-to-late afternoon. Avoid after heavy rain due to surface area run-off.

GPS 39.545654 / 2.619134

Porto Pi

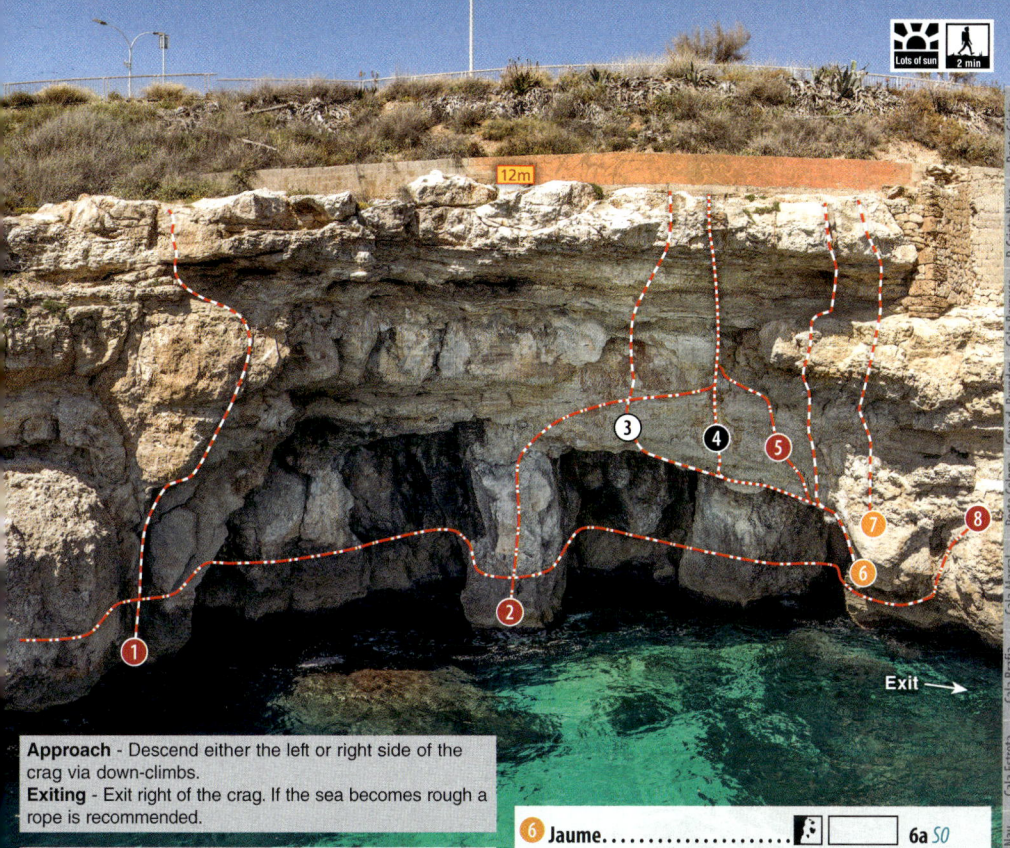

Approach - Descend either the left or right side of the crag via down-climbs.
Exiting - Exit right of the crag. If the sea becomes rough a rope is recommended.

❶ Pepelink........................ 6b S2
The left arch with some good holds until you reach the top. Watch the boulder below.
FA. Miquel Riera early 80s

❷ Pilar 6b S0
Either swim, use a dinghy, or attempt to climb around to the start of this one. Climb the pillar, move right onto the face and then attack the roof at the top.
FA. Miquel Riera early 80s

❸ Mucho mi............. 8b+ S0
Porto Pi's big number cruncher! Starting on the right side of the cove, traverse the lip of the cave and launch out onto the face to cross the line of *Pilar* into a small corner. Power over the roof to finish.
FA. Miquel Riera late 80s

❹ Meca.................. 7b S0
Make an early exit from *Mucho mi* and finish on *Pilar*.
FA. Miquel Riera late 80s

❺ Cuquets 6b S0
Probably the first recorded deep water solo on the island. Start as for *Jaume*, which avoids the hard lip climbing below, to move into the upper part of *Meca*.
FA. Miquel Riera 1978

❻ Jaume................... 6a S0
On the right of the cove. Beware of brittle rock.
FA. Miquel Riera late 70s

❼ Sa primera.............. 6a S0
Right of *Jaume*, climb up to and over the roof.
FA. Miquel Riera late 70s

❽ Cave Traverse .... 6c+ S0
A traverse of the cave in either direction.
FA. Stephen Maginn 17.7.2024

❾ Starter Traverse 6a S0
From the headland, traverse left into the main bay and exit up the gully used to access the other climbs here. Alternatively link into *Sa primera*.
FA. Sarp Akcay 9.10.2022

A small bay to the right of the main area with two fun outings.

❿ Left Traverse 6a S0
A low-level traverse across the right side of the cave to the lip. Exit above.
FA. Sarp Akcay 9.10.2022

⓫ Right-to-Left Traverse ..... 6a+ S0
From the leaning block on the right side of the cave, drop down and trend left up to the lip of the cave. Exit above.
FA. Sarp Akcay 9.10.2022

Mallorca Deep Water Soloing — Route Index

Stars	Grade	Route	Photo	Page
*	6b+	2D 3D		61
*	7b+	Abugraib		120
	7b+	Acuatic		120
**	6b	Adosat		114
*	6a+	Adventure Land		59
**	6b+	Albornoz		115
*	7a	Alcaeda		119
*	6b	Alex's		151
*	6c	Ali muma ye		119
∘∘∘	8b+	Animal Magnetism	23	101
∘∘∘	8c	Animalistic		101
	6b	Anselm		114
**	6b+	Aqua Phobia		150
*	6c	Aquafresh		73
*	6b	Aresta		138
**	6a	Aromes de Margrony		119
	6a	Art God		74
**	6b+	As Good as it Gets	83	84
*	6b+	Asexual		53
**	6c	Aspergilo		118
*	5c	Atom		79
***	7a+	Attack of the Spindly Killer Fish	93	89
*	6c+	Baby Nate		66
*	7b+	Baby Sepia		130
	6b	Bag Puss		119
∘∘	8a	Balam		139
**	7a+	Balsa Boys		98
	7a+	baluart, Es		119
***	7c	Bandito		53
*	5c	Bandy	99	98
	7b	Banyada		120
**	6b	Barques Traverse, The		50
	6b	Batalla de cazalla		112
	6b	BBC		120
**	6a	Beachside Traverse		94
	4a	Big Easy Flake		153
∘∘∘	8a+	Big Mama		57
***	7a	Big XXL		49
∘	8b	Bipolar Ape		100
*	6b	Bird Watching		132
*	5a	Bird Watching Direct		132
***	7a	Bisexual		53
*	6a	Black Jack		80
*	5a	Blue Bikini		80
**	6c	bol.leti, Es		118
*	6b	Bombas		113
**	7a	Bou		116
*	6c	Bounty		92
*	6a+	Braune Gurken		54
	5c	Brazilian Boy, The		111
**	6b	Brazilian Girl, The		110
*	6a+	Broker		119
	6b+	Bull and the Bride, The		85
*	4c	C++		89
*	6a	Cala What?		70
	7a+	Calvía		119
**	6c+	Camp Jogger, The		61
*	4a	Canada		73
*	6b	Cantabrica		120
	6b	Cap torero sense banyas		113
***	7a	Captain Black		88
*	6c	Captain Hook		52
∘∘	8a	Carlos Checa		54
**	7c	Caro Line		85
	6a+	Carpenter		104
	6c+	Catch 22		54
*	7a	Cave Route		89
*	6c+	Cave Traverse		155
**	6b	Chanelance		112
	6a+	Chapman	29	48
**	6c	Check Out	103	102
**	6c+	Cheers Chartle		91
*	7c	Chungulungu		64
*	7a	Cocktail O'Clock		133
	5a	Coldron		89
	6a+	Colomic Irrigation		74
	6a	Coloms		119
*	6c	corna, La		113
	6a+	Cova Descent		50
*	7a+	Cris Rabbit		67
**	7a	Cristo		148
*	7b	Culo Superchulo		64
**	6b	Cuquets		155
	6a	Dead Prawn		72
*	5c	Deep Sea Climbing		153
*	6b	Diedre 1		116
**	6c	Diedre 2		121
**	6a+	Dihedral		130
	5a	Dim Dim		152
	6a	Dimiti		120
**	6b+	Dino Egg Traverse, The		95
*	6b	Dolby		118
	3a	Dolphins are Friendlier than Yaks		74
*	6b	Dominion Wall		61
	6b	Don Simon		113
**	7a	Door, El		52
*	7b+	Double Penetration		49
**	6b	Down		119
*	7a	Dreta		119
**	6c+	Drop Shadow Diseases		49
***	6c+	Drop Zone	62	67
	3a	Ease of Passage, The		153
**	7c	Easyfo		100
*	6b+	Eatsy's Cave		142
*	6b	Efecto especial verbal I		115
	6b	Efecto especial verbal II		115
**	6a	Electric Sky		123
*	6a+	Electron		79
∘∘∘	8b+	Empainada		101
***	6b+	Enter the Kraken	8	102
***	6c+	Entrecot de bicepse		110
**	7b	Erection		49
*	7c+	Escape of Thanatos		100
**	6c	escuela, La		113
**	6c	Escupe la flema		112
**	7a	Espases		120
	6b	Especula		114
∘∘	8a+	Esplendor geometrico		137
**	6c	Estilo Pancho Villa		113
**	6b	ET v Predator		72

Porto Cristo · P. Cristo Novo · Cala Barques · Cova d. Burador · Porto Colom · Cala Marçal · Cala Brafia · Cala Estreta · Cala Sa Nau · Cala Mitjana · Cala Serena · Santanyi · Cala Llombards · Sa Calobra · Port de Soller · Porto Pi

Route Index — Mallorca Deep Water Soloing

Stars	Grade	Route	Photo	Page
	6b	Europa		121
**	7a+	Exhibitionist Finish, The		144
**	6a+	Eye Poker		79
**	6a+	Fat Crab, The	71	72
***	6a+	Felcher, The		144
**	7a+	Filthy Rich		98
☆☆☆	8a+	Follam Balam	134	138
*	5a	Follow the Light		104
*	6b	Force of Nature		85
**	6a+	Fortuna		54
**	4c	Frogger		89
*	7c	From Dusk 'til Dawn		57
**	6b+	Fulcher, The		144
**	7a	Future Barny		64
	7a	Fuut-Lappen		48
*	6b	Galactics		118
	6b	Gasolina		121
**	6a	Geek		98
**	6b	Gen Lock		89
*	6b	Genoveses		49
*	6a+	Given		80
*	6b	Gluon		59
***	7a	Golden Shower	51	50
	7b	Goldene Nase		50
*	7b+	Goldie Hawn		50
*	6b	Golpe bajo		113
*	7b+	Granaten Woman		49
*	7a+	Granaten-Einstieg		49
	4c	Great Escape, The		84
*	5b	Great Sarah Psych!, The		98
**	6a+	Groove Rider		73
	6b	Guais estails		113
	7b	Guantanamo		120
*	6b	Hellraiser		72
***	6c	Hercules		54
**	6b	Hier Kommt Alex		111
**	6a	Higher than the Sun		73
	6a+	Hip-Hop to the Top		73
*	5c	Homerophobia		73
*	7b	Homosexual		53
*	6c+	Horizontal Shuffle		124
*	7b	Hot Chili		53
*	6a	Hoy Voy de Guiri		73
*	6a	Hung Drawn and Quartered		85
☆☆☆	8b	Hupolup Kempf		91
**	6b+	I Live in a Cave	65	66
*	4c	I Tell Thee		89
*	6b	Ikusi Arte		111
***	6b+	Illuminations	1, 105	101
*	6b+	IMAX		61
☆☆☆	8b	Inconvenient Roof, An		85
	7b	It Tastes Like the Sea		151
*	6a+	Italian Riviera, The		59
☆☆	8b	Jackie Brown		57
	6a	Jaume		155
*	6c	Johnnie Walker		98
*	6c+	JTL		48
**	7b	Juanjo Beach		48
**	7b	Juanjo Beach - Left-hand Start		48
**	7b	Kill Bill 1		57
***	7c	Kill Bill 2		57
**	6b	Killer Virgin		88
*	6b+	Klem Beach		50
*	7b+	Kurt Husser		50
*	5c	Lady Boys		73
*	7b	Lama		139
	6a+	Lamancha		123
*	6c	Land that Time Forgot, The		85
	7a+	Le Cash-bomb		48
*	6b+	Left Arete, The		98
*	6b	Left Cave Traverse		52
	6a	Left Cave Traverse - Flake Finish		52
*	5c	Left Side Traverse		143
*	6a	Left Traverse		155
☆	8a	Leistenmatz		48
	7a	Les ajudes		118
*	7a	Linguine	147	151
*	5c	Lion's Head, The		60
*	6b+	Little Blue, The		151
*	5c	Little Fish		89
	6b+	Little Princess		151
*	5c	Little Professor, The		142
*	7a	Llet negra		118
*	7c	Locat matador		137
**	7a+	Long Traverse		85
**	6b+	Losing My Virginity		88
	6b	Lost in Lamancha		123
*	7a+	Lost Property Attrocity		92
*	6c	Low Traverse		98
**	7b	Luciana		64
**	6c+	Mad Professor, The		142
*	6b	Magic Bean Traverse, The		124
	7b+	Malle		121
	6c	Mallorca es fonki		112
*	6a+	Mallorca es funky		110
***	7a	Mallorcan, The		142
☆☆☆	8a	Mamasita		57
*	6a+	Man of Steel		132
	6c	Manca		118
	6b	manicura, La		113
**	6b	Mano negra	107	119
**	6a+	Mapau		119
	6a	Marçal Morceau		74
**	5c	Marçal Traverse, The		74
*	6a+	Maria mirame		61
*	6b	mas fardon, El		113
*	7a	Mataconejos		66
	7b	Maximuscle		101
*	7b	Meca		155
*	7a+	Medalles		118
*	6b	Mega		118
**	6b	Mengen fetge		118
*	6b	Meteoro		119
**	7a+	Metrosexual	12, 18	53
*	6c	Metxicans		149
☆☆	8a+	Mezmerizer		101
	7a	Mi llamo Chris		67
***	6b	Mi primera flinada	125	120
☆☆	8a	Mia Julia		85
*	4a	Michalien		150

Mallorca Deep Water Soloing — Route Index

Stars	Grade	Route	Photo	Page
*	6b+	Midnight Mast.		100
**	6c+	Might of the Stalactite, The	2	49
	6b	Mini me		115
✩✩	8a+	Minitas		131
*	7a+	Mitjana Party		100
***	6c+	Mitjana Party - Left		100
*	6b	Moc		115
**	6b	Mocs i po		115
***	6b+	Mortal Combat	75	72
	6a	Mr. Smith		133
✩✩	8b+	Mucho mi		155
*	7a+	Muscles from Brussels, The		57
*	4c	Naked Germans		133
*	6b+	Neutrino.		79
	5a	Neutron		80
*	6a	New Born		80
***	6b+	New Forms		101
*	7a+	Niagara Will Fall.		66
**	7a	Nip Slip		98
*	7a+	No Man's Land		67
*	7a+	No me puedo quejar		64
*	6b	No Te Rindas		61
*	6a	Nomas		119
*	6b	Nora		113
**	6b+	Notatrocity		91
*	5c	O Hey!		48
✩	8a	O-Ren Ishii		57
**	7a	Oachikas		48
	5c	Oaker's Lab		74
**	6a	Oceans in the Sky		123
*	5a	Odyssey, The		73
*	7b	Omprakash		64
**	6b+	One Tom, One Cup		60
***	6a+	Orange Wall.		94
*	6b	Owl Cave	80	79
**	7a	Pansexual.		53
	7b	papa, Es		118
*	6b	Pasate el microfono.		113
	6a	Passage to the New, A		152
*	7a	pate, Es		118
*	6b	Pepelink.		155
**	7a+	Photon Reverse		78
*	6b	Photon Traverse.		79
*	6b	Pilar		155
*	6c+	placa de Sauron, La		110
*	6a	Planet POB		85
*	5c	Pontas Revenge		122
	6c	Pontas Traverse		130
✩✩✩	9a+	Pontas, Es	126	131
✩	8b+	Pontasaffair		131
✩✩	8c	Pontasaffair - Alt		131
✩✩✩	8c	Pontax		131
*	6a	Pontification.		131
	7a	Pop		118
	6b	Pots		152
	6a	Prawn in the Sun		123
*	6c	Prest		121
***	7a	Princess of Transilvania.		66
**	6c	PSM		149
*	6b	Que escaqueoi		110
*	7c	R-Rodler, The		54
**	7a+	Rabbit is Dead, The.		66
**	6c	Ralph Kaiser's Neue Kleider		50
**	6a	Rasputin		119
*	6a	Rat Dog		74
	6b	Raticida		57
***	6c	Redeemer.	117	110
*	7c	Rene Colo		64
*	7c	Republica Sinestra		148
**	7b	Rest Day		79
*	6c+	Rib Tickler.		102
***	6c+	Rich Bitch.	3, 21	98
*	6a+	Right-to-left traverse		155
	6a	Ritmo Carioca.		111
**	6b+	Ritmo De Samba, A.		111
*	5c	Road Warrior, The		104
*	6b	Rodio		70
	6a	Romani		120
*	6c	Roter Baron		49
	7a	S'aixeta		119
*	7a+	S'atic		66
	7a	Sa fundacio		116
	6c	Sa multa		120
**	6b+	Sa Pose.		143
	6a	Sa primera		155
*	6a	Sa rossaguera		138
*	6c	Sa tangent		137
✩✩	8b	Salty Beverage		91
	6a	Scalfament		91
	6a+	Scalfament 2		91
**	6b	Scorpion	69	72
	6a	Scrunch		122
*	6b	Sense casc		121
*	6b	Setze jutges.		118
*	6c+	She.		50
	7c+	Should I Stay or Should I Go		101
*	6b	Sifon y jena		113
✩✩✩	8a	Sisifo		100
*	7a	Sixty's Silver Surfer		49
✩✩	8a	Smash it in!		53
✩✩✩	8a+	Snatch		54
*	7c	Solecito		53
***	7a	Sóller		119
**	6a+	Sosec		119
*	6a+	Southwest Face.		130
	6c	Span-tastic		79
**	7a	Speed of Light		78
	6b	Spider Salad		139
	6b	Spiders with Chips		139
**	6b+	Squeeze		122
*	6b	Squid		152
*	6a	Starter Traverse		155
***	6c+	Stigmata	81	78
*	6a	Stolen		123
*	6a+	Stop Look and Listen		131
✩✩	8a	Stranger than Paradise		54
***	7b+	Strangers in Paradise.	44, 55	54
	7b+	Submarina		120
**	6c+	Super Sonic.		132
**	7b+	Superguapa.		121
*	6b	Supermanolo		148
*	7b	Supermarket Fantasy		49

Porto Cristo · P. Cristo Novo · Cala Barques · Cova d. Burador · Porto Colom · Cala Marçal · Cala Brafia · Cala Estreta · Cala Sa Nau · Cala Mitjana · Cala Serena · Santanyí · Cala Llombards · Sa Calobra · Port de Soller · Porto Pí

Mallorca Deep Water Soloing

Buttress Index

Stars	Grade	Route	Photo	Page
***	6b	Sweet Serena.		122
	6b	Tacon cubano.		113
**	6b	Tanassa.		149
☆	8a+	Te lo juro por Snoopy.		139
**	6c	Te mando a casa en barco de rejilla.		110
*	7a	Techno Mancore!.		61
**	7a	Tekken 2.		73
*	7b+	Tequila-men.		66
**	6b	Terra.		120
**	5a	Terry-fied.		104
**	6a+	Terry-nova.		104
**	6c	Tevatron.		79
**	6c+	Third Time Lucky.		80
**	6a	Time.		73
*	7a+	Tiramisu.		124
*	6c+	Titan.		67
*	6a	To Infinity.		123
***	6b+	Tokio.		118
*	7a	Topspin.		67
*	6b	Toques.		119
	6b	Toreros muertos I.		115
	6b	Toreros muertos II.		115
	6b	Tort.		120
*	7a+	Tortilla Traverse, The.		119
	7b	Tot petit.		118
	7a	Tower of Power.		50
**	7a+	Toxic Musculinity.		78
☆☆	8a	Trail Hawk.		101
	6c	Tramontana.		149
*	7b	Transexual.		53
***	7a	Transversal.		49
*	6b	Treasure Island.		128
*	6a	Trekin' Herd.		50
*	6a	Trobador.		121
	6a	Two Finger Fun.		123
**	6b	Under a Dark Sky.		92
*	6a+	Up Quark.		79
	6c	Vacaciones en el mar.		112
***	7b	Vadage.		91
	6b	Vinga bou.		118
*	6a	Vino Master.		133
**	6b+	Vip.		119
**	6a+	Virgins are Only Human.		88
	6b	Vuitmil.		114
	5a	Warm.		102
*	6c+	Watch for the Jellies.		54
	6a	Water Logged.		143
*	5c	Wave Machine.		133
***	7a	Wax.	145	144
☆☆☆	8a+	Weather Man - Left-hand, The.		91
☆☆☆	8a+	Weather Man, The.		91
*	7b	Wenga Xavi.		64
**	7a+	Westatrocity.		92
**	7a	Wetter than an Otter's Pocket.		48
**	7b	What a Small World.		88
*	7a+	Without a Paddle.		133
☆☆	8a	Xapapote.		121
	6c	xina, La.		118
***	7a+	xirimollo, Es.		121
	6c	Zafarrancho.		113
*	7a	Zazpigarrena.		110

Buttress Index

Buttress	Page
Adosat, Sector	114
Aqua Wall	151
Bay Area - Super Sonic	132
Bay Area - The Cove	133
Bay Traverses	94
Bay Wall	150
Bombas, Sector	112
Bounty Sector	92
Brazil, Sector	110
Cala Wall	80
Cave (Cala Estreta)	84
Cova Area	48
Cova de ses Puntes	148
Cova del Diablo	34
Dominion Wall	61
Es Pontas	130
Hupolup Kempf Cave	91
Ice Screamers Wall	153
Infinity Wall	123
Kraken Wall	102
Lion's Head	60
Llombards East	138
Llombards West	137
Main Cliff (Cala Marçal)	72
Main Wall (Cala Brafia)	78
Muscles Cave	57
One Tom	60
Pots Wall	152
Prest, Sector	121
Rich Bitch Cave	98
Riviera and Adventure Land	59
Sa Fundiacio Cave	116
Serena Wall	122
Small Headland	74
Snatch Area	54
Sosec, Sector	118
Surfing Bird Area	34
Tarantino Cave	57
Terry Wall	104
The Arena	144
The Cala Wall	74
The Lobster Area	36
The Mouth	143
The Professor Wall	142
Tiramisu, Sector	124
Tort, Sector	120
Tower of Falcons	40
Treasure Island	128
Virgin Area	88
Wall of Illuminations	100
White Noise Area	38

Mallorca Deep Water Soloing — Map and General Index

Access 22	Map Symbols 16
Accommodation 16	New Areas 22
Acknowledgments 9	New Routes 22
Advertisers 9	Opening Times 19
Buttress Index 159	Public Transport 17
Climbing Shops 19	Rainfall 14
Conditions 22	Rockfax Digital 6
Deep Water Solo Grades 24	Rockfax Publications 10
Destination Planner 26	S Grades 24
Destination Planner 26	Safety 25
Flights 14	Shops 19
Gear 22	Splashdowns 25
Getting Around 17	Symbol, Map and Topo Key 7
Getting There 14	Symbols 7
Getting there by Air 14	Temperature 14
Getting there Without Flying 14	The Book 4
Grade Colour Codes 24	Tides 22
Grade Table 24	Topo Key 7
Grades 24	Tourist Information Offices 19
Guiding Services 19	Travel Insurance 14
Introduction 4	UKClimbing Logbooks 6
Jelly Fish 22	Weather 14
Map 16, 160	When to Go 14
Map Key 7	Where to Stay 16

Mountain Rescue

Dial 112 - Ensure you have details of your location and what the incident involves. This number works on any mobile on a Spanish network.

Mallorca
Deep Water Soloing

Text, topos, crag photography by Daimon Beail
Additional crag photography by Mark Glaister
Other photography as credited
Edited by Alan James and Rebecca Ting
Printed in Europe LF Book Services
(ISO 14001 and FSC certified printers)
Distributed by Cordee (cordee.co.uk)

Maps by Alan James
Some maps based on original source data
from openstreetmap.org

Fax70 - ISBN 978 1 873341 19 3

Published by Rockfax in April 2025
© Rockfax 2025

Rockfax is part of UKClimbing Limited
which is an Employee Ownership Trust

All rights reserved. No part of this publication may be reproduced, stored in a retrieval system, or transmitted in any form or by any means, electronic, mechanical, photocopying or otherwise without prior written permission of the copyright owner. A CIP catalogue record is available from the British Library.

We only use paper made from wood fibre from sustainable forests and produced according to ISO 14001 environmental standard.

Cover: Hazel Findlay on *Ejector Seat* (7c) - *p.36* - at Cova del Diablo, Porto Cristo. Photo: Matty Hong

This page: Daimon Beail on *Illuminations* (6b+) - *p.101* - at Cala Mitjana. Photo: Beail Collection

This book belongs to: